PLACEMENT GUIDEBOOK

Table of Contents

TEFL Roadmap to Going Abroad

TEFL Certification

See page 37 on completing your TEFL training with TEFL Institute.

First Things First

Go to pages 13 – 15 to learn the first steps of getting organized to go abroad. Learn valuable tips for setting up your email, voicemail, etc.

Introductory Documents

Check out pages 35 – 36 for a complete checklist of documents you may need to go abroad. Pages 51 – 61 contain our highly informative International Resume Writing Guide.

Select Your Country

Start reading on page 71 to learn about salary, benefits, and teaching opportunities around the world.

Start Job Search

Are you ready to begin your job search? Start online. We have an entire list of online job boards and websites. Go to page 93.

Schedule Interview

Pages 62-67 tell you all about the do's and don'ts of interviewing for an ESL job abroad. We have loads of questions you can ask your school.

Accept a Job Offer

If you like the job offer accept it, or if you have questions begin reading on page 67 of the Guidebook for more help.

GO ABROAD

Its time to pack, buy airline tickets and more. Go to www.teflinstitute.com to download your free "*Travel and Safety Guidebook.*"

Introduction

Thank you for choosing TEFL Institute. We are a premier international TEFL training organization based in Chicago, Illinois USA. Our courses prepare you to teach English abroad. We provide job placement assistance to course graduates. By now you have probably begun or completed your TEFL Certification course and you would like to know the next steps to finding an English teaching job abroad. This guidebook serves as a step-by-step process to getting an English teaching job and can be used as a reference tool for future use.

Our TEFL training courses are offered at Roosevelt University, Global Crossroads, English World, JourneyEast, Canadian Educational Ventures, and numerous other organizations. In addition, we provide TEFL training directly to students with our internationally recognized TEFL courses. Classes are available online, on the weekend, or at various international locations around the world.

ABOUT THE GUIDEBOOK

The guidebook contains nine (9) chapters covering everything from resume writing and salary information by country to a school directory with thousands of contacts and what to do once you get the job.

You may examine each chapter in order or move from one chapter to another as needed. This guidebook was developed for both uses in mind.

Ti Gibbs wrote much of the original content presented in this book. Ti is the President of TEFL Institute and has traveled extensively abroad.

The Guidebook's first chapter is called "First Things First." It is a short list of the first things you should do before you begin your job search abroad. In Chapter Two you will find contact information for TEFL Institute. Chapter Three is titled "Job Search process" in which we give you a step-by-step procedure for self-placement activities or using the services of TEFL Institute.

About the Guidebook

In Chapter Four you will find a full and comprehensive checklist of materials your schools may request from you, it is called "Material Checklist." Chapter Five reviews the steps in "Completing your TEFL Certification" course. Chapter Six is a simple but effective "International Resume Guide" and Chapter Seven offers helpful information you will need regarding your "Interviews and Contracts" abroad. Chapter Eight provides a detailed "Country Guide" and Chapter Nine is a "List of Job Boards and Websites" that you can use as resources.

	Online	In-Person	Hours	Placement Services Provided
TEFL Professional	X		120	TEFL Institute offers job placement assistance including resume, cover letter and job search advice and coordination.
TEFL International		X	120	TEFL Institute and onsite staff offer placement assistance including resume, cover letter and job search advice and coordination.
Roosevelt University	X		120	TEFL Institute coordinates your placement.
TEFL Basic	X		50	Self-directed placement, you will use the placement guide and find your job without TEFL Institute's assistance.
TEFL Seminar		X	20	Self-directed placement, you will use the placement guide and find your job without TEFL Institute's assistance.

Please note: TEFL Institute provides job placement assistance to any course graduate seeking to teach English for one year or longer in: Chile, China, Japan, Korea, or Taiwan.

Short Term Teaching Projects (1 to 3 months)

We offer short-term English teaching abroad assignments to all TEFL Course graduates through our Summer Programs only. The programs are offered at no additional costs to all TEFL Course graduates by TEFL Institute. Since these are group programs and you pay no additional fees to participate, we ask that all participants attend the Chicago Orientation for their country. Programs are offered in Argentina, Chile, China, and Spain. Other countries may be added, consult your TEFL Advisor for the most current information on these programs.

Requirements of employers vary from country to country and from school to school too, so although there may be many jobs advertised for a particular country, you may find that you do not match the profile they are looking for. The majority of employers in the European Union will only accept TEFL instructors with at least a 120 hour TEFL certification.

WHERE CAN I TEACH?

There are English teaching opportunities in just about every country around the world. The demand for English teachers is much greater in some countries than in others. Take a look at job boards such as http://www.eslbase.com/jobs/ to get an idea of some of the countries where work is available at the moment.

Most employers in the western countries of the European Union (EU) such as France, Italy, and Spain, will only accept EU citizens for advance interviews. Most jobs in Asia and Europe are only available for people who have a BA degree. Many schools in some countries in the Middle East require a high level qualification, several years of teaching experience, and will not recruit newly qualified teachers.

Having said this, the ample number of opportunities available means that there is something for almost everyone.

There are ESL/EFL teaching jobs in almost every country and probably even in your home community. The most jobs available with the highest pay for beginning EFL teachers are in Asia. The chart on the next page gives an estimated breakdown on the percentage of EFL jobs worldwide.

Teaching Projects (1 to 12 months)

THE PERCENTAGE OF EFL JOBS BY REGION WORLDWIDE

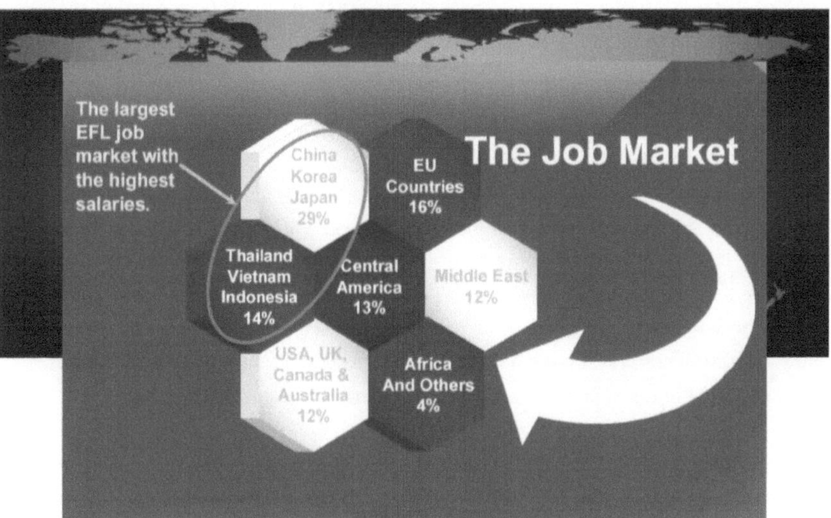

JOB MARKET HIGHLIGHTS BY REGION TABLE

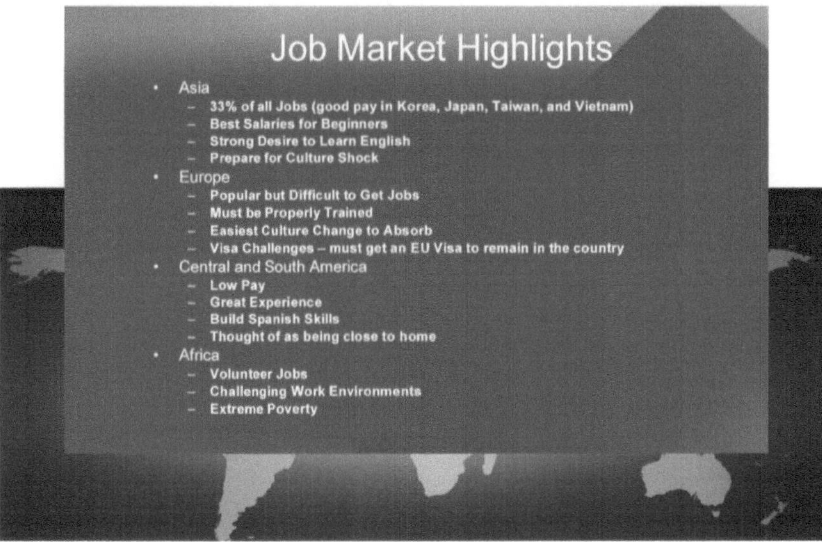

Teaching Projects (1 to 12 months)

Teachers can expect to be paid at the local prevailing wage rate in a country. It is good to be familiar with the median or typical salary for teachers in a particular country before you go. In many developing or emerging countries teachers are paid only a fraction of what they may earn in the United States, Canada, United Kingdom or other western countries. However, your schools will try to pay you a living wage or provide you with housing and a small stipend.

The poorer or less developed countries cannot afford to pay someone to come and teach English. As such they are seeking volunteers. As a volunteer you will pay for much of your own housing and living expenses. In some cases, you will pay those monies directly to your host organization. The host organization will use those monies to help defray the costs of operating their programs. It will cover the cost of the personnel that answered your emails and telephone calls, picked you up at the airport, and served as your escort while you were in the country. These costs have to be met somehow and for many poorer countries, the generosity of volunteers is necessary in the running of their programs.

We have tried to give you a representative sample of pay packages by countries or regions around the world. As a general rule of thumb, in many African, Central America, and Southeast Asia countries you will be offered volunteer only positions. In the other regions of the world you will be paid the local wage rate for that country. It will be enough for you to live on but it will not make you rich.

HOW DO I FIND A JOB?

The most common way to find an English Teaching job abroad is through an online EFL/ESL job board or employment website. When you find a job that interests you submit your international resume or Curriculum Vitae (CV). Be sure to check for grammatical or spelling errors.

If you fit the school's profile, they will contact you to arrange an interview. It is usually a telephone interview that will last about 30 to 60 minutes with the school's Recruiting Manager or the School Director.

In the chapter called, "Getting the Interview", we go through some of the common questions you may be asked during the interview, as well as some questions you may want to ask the interviewer or a teacher currently at the school.

Many schools hire recruiting agencies or agents to find their candidates. Others will advertise in the local newspapers and "expat" magazines, as well as just relying on word

of mouth from people searching for English teaching jobs abroad. If your job search is in a country you can expect a face-to-face interview. Recruitment agencies often still advertise on TEFL recruitment websites (agencies are most common in countries such as South Korea or China). The advantage of agencies is that once they have your resume or CV on file they can continue to contact you for any suitable job that may arise in the future.

SALARY: HOW MUCH WILL I BE PAID?

You are paid by your employer or school. Your salary is paid in accordance with the local prevailing wage rates in that country. You can expect to earn enough to live a comfortable middle class existence for that country. Europe and Latin America teachers make enough on their 25 hours a week to break even. You should make enough for your standard expenses of housing, food, transportation and a little pocket money. In Asia and the wealthier Middle East countries teachers typically save 30-50% of their salary. Most teachers will take on private tutoring which is often available to command double the hourly wage you are making at your school. This is very common and teachers find this money goes a long way for savings or for fun travel money.

WHAT IS FULL TIME WORK FOR AN ENGLISH TEACHER?

For an English teacher abroad, the TEFL Institute will use this definition of full time work:

- A full time teacher typically teaches at least 20 hours a week although you may teach as many as 35 hours per week in some countries. Typical teaching is 25 teaching hours with an additional 10-12 hours a week for lesson and material preparation. Pay is usually based on actual teacher class contact time, not lesson planning.
- Full time teachers should earn enough pay to support themselves in a country. There are hundreds of thousands of teachers around the world and they all support themselves financially by their profession.

HOUSING WORLDWIDE

Often in a larger city, you will live in an apartment. You will be assisted to find an apartment by your school or you may share an apartment with another teacher. You will pay for your own housing out of your salary; the cost is up to you. Some schools may offer you a place to stay (apartment or dorm) for a few days to several months until you locate an apartment. You should be prepared to have money for a security deposit and first month's rent just as you would move in the US.

If in a small city, the school will often arrange a home stay for you with a local family. You will have your own bedroom and share the home with a local family that is accustomed to foreign teachers. The housing cost will either be taken from your pay and forwarded to the family or you will pay the family directly

MEDICAL INSURANCE

When you go abroad, you need to have your own international medical insurance. Some countries like Korea and Japan, for example, may offer national medical insurance with their teaching contracts. In these cases, both the teacher and the school will pay into the system. The teacher will be on the national health insurance plan. Be sure to ask your school about this possibility and their recommendations. It is important for everyone to have international medical insurance. This applies to those who may be covered by their schools on a national health plan as well. Keep in mind the plans may take a little while to set up. Therefore it is important for you to do some research into the international medical insurance options before you leave your home country. There are a lot of different companies out there. Internet research is your best tool. Among the larger providers are HTH Worldwide, Global Health and STA travel. Visit their websites and research your options. It is important to determine the best for yourself given your needs.

START UP MONEY – CASH IN HAND STARTING A JOB:

Money is needed for first month's rent, deposit, food, and transportation costs plus some extra money for emergency.

Recommended amount of $1,000-$1,500 on average to cover 4-6 weeks of housing, food, and transportation before your first paycheck is cashed.

PASSPORT AND VISAS

Remember also that all participants must have a passport valid for at least six months after the end of the program in which you are participating. Processing a passport can take six weeks to three months now that the US has passed new international travel laws. If you have a passport, check that it will be valid for the period in question. Do not delay your application if you are waiting to receive a passport, but make sure we know you are obtaining one. Your hiring school will provide you with information needed to obtain a work visa if necessary. Non U.S. applicants are responsible for making passport and visa arrangements but should consult with our office if they need help.
To obtain a US passport go to the State Department website:
http://travel.state.gov/passport/passport_1738.html
You can also obtain a passport through the US Post Office, www.usps.com.

Teaching Projects (1 to 12 months)

SALARY GRID BY COUNTRY

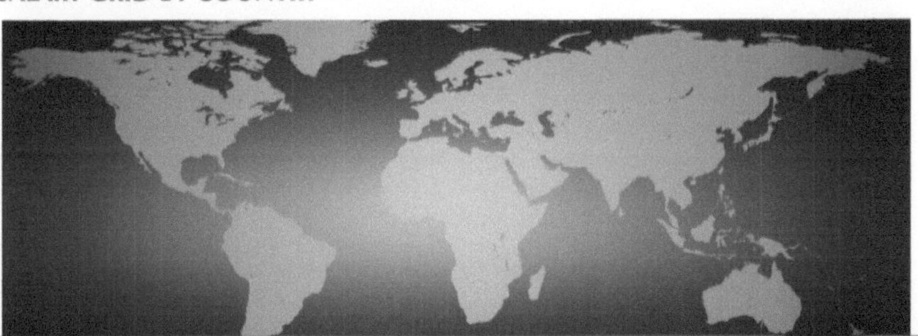

Country	Lenth of Contract	Best Time To Start	Salary	Housing	flights paid	Visa Issues
Argentina	6 & 12 Months	Mid Aug - Early Oct Late Feb - Early April	$ 100 USD per month	free homestay and apartment	no	no visa necessary
Brazil	3, 6 & 12 Months	Jan, March Aug- Oct	12-14 R /hour or 850 R + housing	homestay, apartment, recidenece house	no	3 months tourist visa, renew it
Chile	6 & 12 Months	Mid Aug - Early Oct Late Feb - Early April	$ 500 - 800 USD month	pay for your own apartment $ 200 / month	no	no visa necessary
China	6 & 12 Months	anytime	$ 500 - 800 USD month	apartment free	some	tourist visa 30 days then convert to work visa
Costa Rica	6 & 12 Months	Feb - March Aug - Oct	$ 5 USD/ hour do hours week	pay for your own apartment	no	none
France	6 & 12 Months	Feb - Aprils (march is best) oct is best	$ 12 Eu / hour	pay for your own apartment $ 600 / month	no	more than 3 months need student visa
Spain	6 & 12 Months	Feb - Aprils (march is best) oct is best	$ 12 Eu / hour	pay for your own apartment $ 600 / month	no	more than 3 months need student visa
S. Korea	12 months	every month	$ 1800 - 2000 / month	apartment free	yes	work visa, 6 weeks to get
Taiwan	12 Months	every month	$ 1,600 - 1,800 month	apartment free	some	tourist visa 30 days then convert to work visa
Thailand	6 & 12 Months	every month	$ 800 USD	apartment free	reimbur se	tourist visa 30 days then convert to work visa
Uruguay	6 & 12 Months	Mid Aug - Early Oct Late Feb - Early April	homestay $ 100 usd	housing free	no	no visa necessary
Vietnam	6 & 12 Months	every month	$ 1,100 $1,800 month $ 1,400 ave	$ 150 - 200 shared apartment	few	tourist visa 30 days then convert to work visa

Disclaimer: We believe this chart is representative of the typical salary novice EFL teachers may earn teaching English abroad. Your individual school will determine your actual pay package. Some will pay more and some will pay less, your final pay is determined by your school

Teaching Projects (1 to 12 months)

Another option is to travel to a country first and look for work when you are there. There are advantages and disadvantages to this. On the plus side, some schools are more likely to hire you if they have met and interviewed you in person and you are already established in the area. Some schools rely entirely on teachers walking in off the street in search of work. On the other hand, there is a risk in spending a lot of time and money with no guarantee of finding a job, particularly if it is your first job and you have chosen a country where many schools require several years of experience.

IS THERE ANYTHING I SHOULD BE AWARE OF IN A SCHOOL?

The great majority of schools are reputable businesses, and except for the inevitable mishaps and inconveniences (broken photocopiers, cultural misunderstandings, etc.), most contracts go without a hitch. But of course, as in any other profession or industry, there are some schools out there who are not reputable, and who seek to take advantage of unsuspecting teachers with more serious consequences than a lack of paper to make photocopies. If you are unlucky enough to encounter one of these schools, or worse, buy a plane ticket, travel to the country and start work, it can be too late by the time you find out that something is amiss. In these instances it is best to quit and find a new school as quickly as possible.

Remember you are not in your home country and taking the time to get even is usually not the best option when you are living abroad. We highly recommend that you learn from the experience and move quickly to find a new teaching job abroad.

The most important thing is to do your research before accepting any offer of employment. Talk to other teachers, join TEFL forums, and do an internet search for the name of the school.

Teaching Projects (1 to 12 months)

AM I ELIGIBLE?

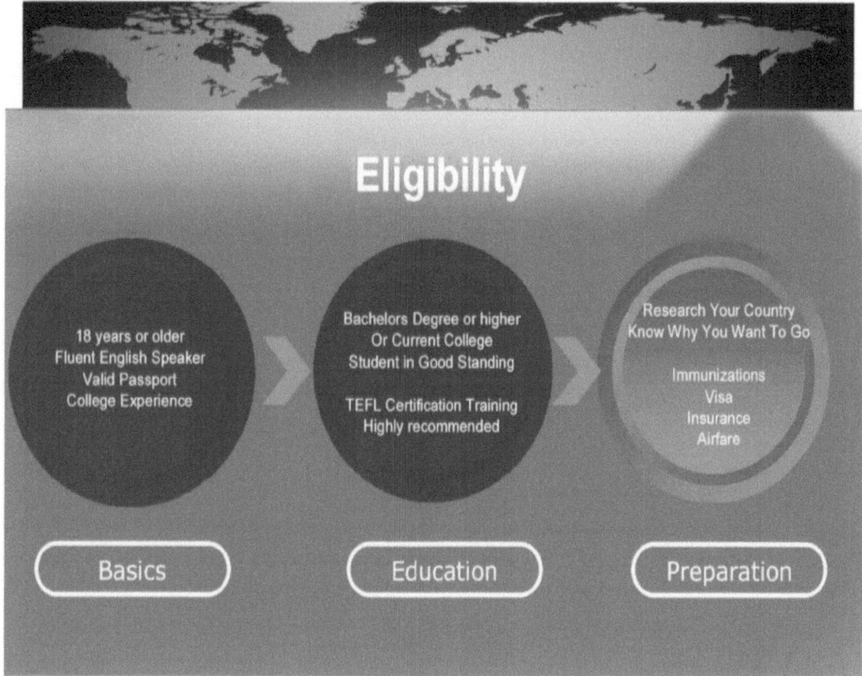

Disclaimer: This information is presented by TEFL Institute, your schools may have other requirements that you will need to meet.

Teaching Projects (1 to 12 months)

WHAT IS THE RESPONSIBILITY OF THE TEFL INSTITUTE GRADUATE?

- Know where you want to go. Research it and be prepared for a professional interview on the phone. Many students do not know which country they wish to work in at the time of TEFL class registration. But, it is important to be clear about as you start your job search abroad.
- Know the best hiring periods. Review our literature as it contains our best determination on peak hiring times. There are often jobs available during non peak hiring seasons but to ensure your highest rate of success we recommend you go during the peak hiring season.
- Prepare a professional International resume following the suggested guidelines the TEFL Institute offers.
- Have photos of you looking professional, neat and clean. This is a representation of you to a hiring committee.
- You should proactively search for jobs on your own via job boards and contact schools through the TEFL Institute Worldwide School Directory.

WHAT TEFL INSTITUTE DOES NOT DO

- It is important that the TEFL Institute student be clear of what is NOT the responsibility of the TEFL Institute. The TEFL Institute is a TEFL training organization that offers job placement assistance and advice. Your tuition payment covers the normal cost of administering your course and it does not include fees for job placement.
- TEFL Institute does not assign you a job that you must take, we are not the military or Peace Corp. We have job contacts in countries that we can put you in touch with to interview for an English teaching job abroad. We give advice and assistance, you make the job decisions.
- We do not guarantee a job with any particular employer, only an employer can offer a job guarantee. Our school contacts want to hire our TEFL trained teachers but you need to have a successful interview and provide all required work documentation that the school requests.
- We do not order your supporting documents for you (transcripts, background checks, letters of reference, etc). You will stand in line at the consulate or handle any of your work paperwork.
- We do not act as an intermediary between you and the school in contract negotiations or handling paperwork or work visas.
- We also do not pay your salary, the school will pay you when you work for them.

First Things First

We recommend five things first before you begin your job search. Of course there are other things to do but before you begin those, it is time to get your communication system in order. You will need email accounts, a voicemail, and a reliable mailing address in place.

Email Accounts

Set up at least two email accounts. One account can serve as your primary account and the other as the back-up account. The accounts will need to be two different services. There are many "free" email accounts services available such as "Yahoo!", "MSN", "Google" and others.

Include information about both accounts on your resume materials and all correspondence materials. At times one email service may restrict content and you may not receive vital information in time. This is not your fault or the senders, the internet may not be as reliable as advertised. Some companies are only trying to protect your computer from a virus attack and they will block certain emails. While no system is fool proof, they are trying to protect your computer and you will need to tell them which emails are safe and which ones are not.

Also, it is a good idea to check your "junk" mail folders from time to time in case emails are being directed into those folders.

Reliable Mailing Address

It is important to have a reliable mailing address that is consistent for the duration of your job search abroad. If you plan to move during your job search gain permission from your parents, relatives, or friends to use one of their addresses.

Time Zone

It is important to know the time zone differences between your home location and the school location. This will help you avoid receiving calls at odd hours or leaving messages when the person you are trying to reach is not available.

First Things First

Voicemail Setup

Its time to set up your voicemail or to clean it up. Eliminate any music and get right to the point. If you have an alternate telephone number or pager that you want someone to call include it in the message. An example greeting could be:

"Hi, this is John Jones. I am not available at this time please feel free to leave a message at the sound of the beep. Or, I can be reached on my cell phone at (555) 555-5555. Thank you for calling."

Digitizing Your Documents

You may be asked to pull together a number of documents for your school such as resume, cover letter, transcripts, college diploma, insurance papers, and more. The first step is to turn all of your paper documents into digital media. You can do this with the use of a scanner.

If you don't own a scanner, visit Kinko's or another similar store to use theirs. Scan your materials and begin saving them for use as needed.

Naming Conventions

Naming your documents is an important step. This little step can help insure that your files are not lost or confused with someone else.

a. Save your resume and cover letter as Word files ending in .doc

b. Save any scanned materials as .jpg or .jpeg files

c. Name your files in the following manner: "Lastname, Firstname Kindofdocument.ext"

For a resume: Jones, John Resume.doc

For a cover letter: Jones, John Cover Letter.doc

For a photo: Jones, John Photo. jpg

For a transcript: Jones, John Transcript.jpg

For a diploma: Jones, John Diploma.jpg

First Things First

Prepare Introductory Materials
Now it is time to introduce yourself to your potential employers by emailing or faxing to your school:

- TEFL Certificate
- Reference Letter from TEFL Institute
- Cover Letter
- International Resume
- Photos

Included in this guidebook are examples of each document.

Contact Your Potential Employer
Once you have selected the country in which you desire to live, work and teach English, it is important to contact as many potential employers as you can.

- English Language Schools Abroad
- Recruiters
- Agents
- Governmental Agencies
- Nonprofits
- Public School systems

You can find numerous employers through the various online job banks or other informational portals.

Contacting TEFL Institute

TEFL Institute
1906 W. Irving Park Road
Chicago, IL 60613 USA

Main: (773) 880-5141
Fax: (773) 880-5940
Website: www.teflinstitute.com
Email: studentservices@teflinstitute.com

Job Search Process

This guidebook is useful for TEFL Professional graduates (those utilizing TEFL Institute Placement Services) and other TEFL course graduates (those conducting self-placement).

I. TEFL PROFESSIONAL GRADUATES

Your placement process will take a minimum of 90 days to complete. It will be conducted by TEFL Institute. If you wish the TEFL Institute to assist in job placement in one of the countries listed in the table on page 19, you must follow these procedures:

Steps	Your Action Steps
1	Contact us at least 3 months prior to your intended start date. If you are going to teach in Chile, China, Korea, Japan, Taiwan or Vietnam, email your resume and photos to TEFL Institute. If you are not teaching in these countries email your materials to your school.
2	If you email us documents we will forward your resume and photos to the school or recruiter via email.
3	Typically, the recruiter or school will contact you via email.
4	You will set up a phone interview and discuss the details directly with the school or recruiter and not with TEFL Institute.
5	Please ask all of the questions you need be answered in order to feel comfortable and confident before accepting a job.
6	If you both agree to accept the job it is your responsibility to follow through with all the paperwork and arrangements necessary for the work, visa, or hiring agreement terms.
7	You will forward all required documentation directly to the hiring school and work out all housing, salary, and benefit details directly with the school, not with the TEFL Institute.

Job Search Process

DOCUMENTS NEEDED FROM YOU (ACCEPTED BY EMAIL ONLY):

Cover Letter

Cover Letter includes:

- When you expect to depart for your country
- How long you would like to live and teach there
- When do you expect to leave
- Any pertinent information regarding you. Some examples would be:
    - If you are married and traveling with your spouse and children
    - If you are traveling with a pet
    - If you have a disability such as blindness or require the use of a wheelchair
    - Specific skills you may have such as business, medical, or legal experience that would improve your value to work with corporate clients

International Resume

Please review the chapter in this guide on International Resumes for examples and detailed instructions on how to prepare an International Resume.

Photos

You will need to submit to your school two (2) photos:

- Head Shot
- Body Shot

Statement of Purpose

Please prepare a Statement of Purpose using 250 words or less. In this statement be clear about:

- Your commitment to teaching English abroad. Reference your TEFL Certificate as proof.
- Your interest in the culture, language, and customs of the country and desire to make new friends and associates.
- The length of time you are prepared to stay. If you are applying for a 12 month job, you will want to say that you plan to remain for a year or longer in the country.

DOCUMENTS CAN BE ACCEPTED BY EMAIL ONLY

Job Search Process

PLACEMENT COUNTRIES TABLE*

	Countries			
TEFL Institute – free placement	Chile Taiwan	China Vietnam	Japan	Korea
Summer Only	Chile	China	Spain	
Volunteer Only	Chile Nepal	Ghana Tanzania	India	Kenya
TEFL Institute School Contacts Available	Costa Rica Indonesia Russia	Estonia Mexico Spain[3]	Germany Peru Turkey	Honduras Poland Uruguay
Use the Guidebook	All Countries			

*The countries listed on this table are subject to change please contact TEFL Institute for the most current list of placement countries.

Teachers must be able to pass any required background, criminal, or educational screenings that is required by their future employer or host organization.

Job Search Process

TEFL INSTITUTE SCHOOL CONTACTS

TEFL Institute conducts a thorough screen of each partner school. It includes a survey with over 50 questions along with requests for photos and testimonials. Every step is taken to help insure TEFL course graduates are placed at highly reputable schools and organizations. Candidates are given contacts at the school and you are to email your cover letter, resume, photo, and statement of purpose directly to that school.

GUIDELINES FOR PLACEMENT ASSISTANCE

To obtain our help you must meet the eligibility requirements for that country. If not, we will ask you to consider another country where we can help you obtain an English teaching job.

TIMELINES AND DUE DATES

We need a minimum of 90 days to conduct your job search. Unfortunately, if you request an earlier departure date or cannot give us enough time conduct your job search, you must conduct a self-placement.

TEFL INSTITUTE CONTACTS

Please note that any and all contacts provided to you by TEFL Institute during this job placement process have undergone an extensive review process. We believe them to be highly reliable and dependable. Many of the recruiters and agents have been with us since our inception.

Some will simply hire you based on our recommendation although we discourage such practices. This is because our previous graduates are outstanding, dedicated, and committed teachers. They have taught at an outstanding level and because they fulfill the duties as well as the duration of their contracts.

We ask that you make every effort to return their email messages and telephone calls in a timely fashion.

Once we have turned you over to a contact. All future contacts will be made between you and the school, recruiter or agent and not TEFL Institute. TEFL Institute does not negotiate school contracts, set up air flights, housing or other matters.

Job Search Process

OUR PLEDGE TO YOU

Our pledge to you, if you are dissatisfied with your placement school, TEFL Institute will help you find a new school. In addition, we will explain to your school why you are leaving to give them an opportunity for improvement (if needed).

TEACHER PAY

As a teacher you will be paid at the local prevailing wage rate in that county. Please see the tables on pages 22-25 for more information on salaries and the best time to find an English teaching job abroad.

Asia

Country	Peak Hiring Seasons	Typical Contract Length	Typical Students	Average Monthly Cost of Living in Local Currency	Average Monthly Salary in Local Currency	Average Monthly Cost of Living in USD	Average Monthly Salary in $ USD	Estimated Start-up Costs *	Housing	Reimbursed Airfare	Visa Info	Degree Requirement	Interview Procedures
Cambodia	Year Round	6 & 12 months	Adults, Children	450-600 $ USD	450-600 $ USD	450-600 $ USD	450-600 $ USD	700-900 $ USD	Self-pay, Housing advice provided by employer	No	Tourist visa convert to work visa	BA and No BA	Face-to-face in destination country
China	Year Round	6 &12 months	Adults, Children	2,000-2,800 RMB **Plus housing**	4,000-6,000 RMB **Plus housing**	300-400 $ USD **Plus housing**	600-800 USD plus free housing. **Can save up to 250-300 USD/Mo**	500-600 $ USD	**Free Housing or Housing Subsidy**	Yes	Work visa in advance or Tourist visa convert to work visa	BA preferred, No BA required depending on location	Phone, email in advance
Hong Kong	Year Round	12 months	Adults, Children	15,000-20,000 HKD	18,000-40,000 HKD	2,300-5,000 $ USD	2,300-3,000 USD. **Can save up to 500-600 USD/Mo**	2,000-2,500 $ USD	Self-pay, Housing advice provided by employer	Sometimes	Work visa in advance	BA required	Phone, email in advance
Indonesia	Year Round	12 months	Adults, Children	6,000,000 - 9,000,000 IDR	7,500,000 - 11,000,000 IDR	600-1,000 $ USD	800-1,200 USD. **Can save up to 250-300 USD/Mo**	600-1,000 $ USD	Self-pay, Housing advice provided by employer	Sometimes	Work visa in advance	Most BA and some no BA	Phone, email in advance
Malaysia	Year Round	12 months	Adults, Children	3,000 – 6,000 MRY	4,000 – 8,000 MRY	900-1,800 $ USD	1,200-2,300 USD. **Can save up to 300-600 USD/Mo**	900-1,800 $ USD	Self-pay, Housing advice provided by employer	No	Work visa in advance	Most BA and some no BA	Phone, email in advance
Japan	Year Round	12 months	Adults, Children	150,000 – 200,000 JPY	250,000 - 280,000 JPY	1,800 – 2,800 $ USD	2,500-2,800 USD. **Can save up to 600-800 USD/Mo**	2,600-4,200 $ USD	Self-pay, Housing advice provided by employer	No	Work visa in advance	BA required	Interview in US, Canada, UK 3 -6 months in advance
Singapore	Year Round	12 months	Adults, Children	3,000 – 3,500 SGD	3,300 – 4,200 SGD	2,100 – 2,500 $ USD	2,400–3,000 USD **Can save up to 300-500 USD/Mo**	2,100-2,500 $ USD	Self-pay, Housing advice provided by employer	No	Work visa in advance	BA required	Phone, email in advance
South Korea	Year Round	12 months	Adults, Children	800,000 - 1,200,000 KRW **Plus housing**	1,800,000 – 2,400,000 KRW **Plus housing**	700-1,000 $ USD **Plus housing**	1,600-1,800 USD Plus free Housing. **Can save up to 1,000 USD/Mo**	700-1,000 $ USD	**Free Housing or Housing Subsidy**	Yes	Work visa in advance	BA required	Phone, email in advance
Taiwan	Year Round	12 months	Adults, Children	32,000 – 46,000 TWD	46,000 – 68,000 TWD	1,000 – 1,400 $ USD	1,400-2,100 USD. **Can save up to 500-600 USD/Mo**	1,000-1,400 $ USD	Self-pay, Housing advice provided by employer	No	Tourist visa convert to work visa or work visa in advance	AA or BA required	Phone, email in advance
Thailand	Year Round	12 months	Adults, Children	15,000 – 25,000 THB	25,000 – 35,000 THB	500-750 $ USD	750-1,000 USD. **Can save up to 150-250 USD/Mo**	750-1,100 $ USD	Self-pay, Housing advice provided by employer	No	Work visa or tourist visa depending on employer	Most BA and some no BA	Most face-to-face in destination country; Some phone and email in advance
Vietnam	Year Round	12 months	Adults, Children	700-900USD	1,200-1,800 $ USD	700-900 $ USD	1,200-1,800 USD. **Can save up to 500-600 USD/Mo**	1,050-1,350 $ USD	Self-pay, Housing advice provided by employer	No	Tourist visa convert to work visa or work visa in advance	BA required	Most face-to-face in destination country; Few phone and email in advance

Latin America

Country	Peak Hiring Seasons	Typical Contract Length	Typical Students	Average Monthly Cost of Living in Local Currency	Average Monthly Salary in Local Currency	Average Monthly Cost of Living in USD	Average Monthly Salary in $ USD	Approximate Start-up Costs*	Housing	Reimbursed Airfare	Visa Info	Degree Requirement	Interview Procedures
Argentina	Feb - Mar, July - Aug	6 & 12 months	Adults	1,500-2,500 ARS	1,500-2,500 ARS	400-600 $ USD	400-600 $ USD	600-900 $ USD	Self-pay, Housing advice provided by employer	No	Tourist Visa	No BA required	Face-to-face in destination country
Bolivia	Feb - Mar, July - Aug	6 & 12 months	Adults	2,800-4,200 BOB	2,800-4,200 BOB	400-600 $ USD	400-600 $ USD	600-900 $ USD	Self-pay, Housing advice provided by employer	No	Tourist Visa	BA and No BA	Face-to-face in destination country
Brazil	Feb - Mar, July - Aug	6 & 12 months	Adults	1,200-2,000 BRL	1,200-2,000 BRL	700-1,100 $ USD	700-1,100 $ USD	1,050-1,650 $ USD	Self-pay, Housing advice provided by employer	No	Tourist Visa	BA required in many	Most face-to-face in destination country; Some phone and email in advance
Chile	Feb - Mar, July - Aug, Summer Programs in public schools	6 & 12 months	Adults, Children with MOE	250,000-430,000 CLP	250,000-430,000 CLP	500-800 $ USD	500-800 $ USD	750-1,200 $ USD	Self-pay, Housing advice provided by employer	No	Tourist Visa or work visa	BA required in most	Many face-to-face in destination country; Some phone and email in advance
Colombia	Feb - Mar, July - Aug	6 & 12 months	Adults	950,000-1,700,000 COP	950,000-1,700,000 COP	500-900 $ USD	500-900 $ USD	750-1,350 $ USD	Self-pay, Housing advice provided by employer	No	Tourist Visa	BA and No BA	Face-to-face in destination country
Costa Rica	Jan-Feb, Jun-July	6 & 12 months	Adults	300,000-360,000 CRC	300,000-360,000 CRC	500-600 $ USD	500-600 $ USD	750-900 $ USD	Self-pay, Housing advice provided by employer	No	Tourist Visa	BA and No BA	Many face-to-face in destination country; Some phone and email in advance
Ecuador	Feb - Mar, July - Aug	6 & 12 months	Adults	400-600 $ USD	400-600 $ USD	400-600 $ USD	400-600 $ USD	600-900 $ USD	Self-pay, Housing advice provided by employer	No	Tourist Visa	BA and No BA	Face-to-face in destination country
Mexico	Jan, Feb, Jun, July, Aug	6 & 12 months	Adults, Children	7,800-9,000 MXN	7,800-9,000 MXN	600-700 $ USD	600-700 $ USD	900-1,050 $ USD	Self-pay, Housing advice provided by employer	No	Tourist Visa. Some work visa	No BA required	Many face-to-face in destination country; Some phone and email in advance
Panama	Feb - Mar, July - Aug	6 & 12 months	Adults	700-900 $ USD	700-900 $ USD	700-900 $ USD	700-900 $ USD	1,050-1,350 $ USD	Self-pay, Housing advice provided by employer	No	Tourist Visa	No BA required	Face-to-face in destination country
Peru	Feb - Mar, July - Aug	3, 6 & 12 months	Adults	1,700-2,300 PEN	1,700-2,300 PEN	600-800 $ USD	600-800 $ USD	900-1,200 $ USD	Self-pay, Housing advice provided by employer	No	Tourist Visa	No BA required	Many face-to-face in destination country; Some phone and email in advance
Uruguay	Feb - Mar, July - Aug	6 & 12 months	Adults	8,500-12,800 UYU	8,500-12,800 UYU	400-600 $ USD	400-600 $ USD	600-900 $ USD	Self-pay, Housing advice provided by employer	No	Tourist Visa	No BA required	Face-to-face in destination country

Europe

Country	Peak Hiring Seasons	Typical Contract Length	Typical Students	Average Monthly Cost of Living in Local Currency	Average Monthly Salary in Local Currency	Average Monthly Cost of Living in $ USD	Average Monthly Salary in $ USD	Approximate Start-up Costs*	Housing	Reimbursed Airfare	Visa Info	Degree Requirement	Interview Procedures
Austria	Sept & Jan	10 & 12 months	Adults	1,800-2,500 Euro	1,800-2,500 Euro	2,600-3,700 $ USD	2,600-3,700 $ USD	3,900-5,500 $ USD	Self-pay, Housing advice provided by employer	No	Tourist Visa, EU Citizenship	BA required	Face-to-face in destination country
Belgium	Sept & Jan	10 & 12 months	Adults	1,600-2,000 Euro	1,600-2,000 Euro	2,400-3,000 $ USD	2,400-3,000 $ USD	3,600-4,500 $ USD	Self-pay, Housing advice provided by employer	No	Tourist Visa, EU Citizenship	BA required	Face-to-face in destination country
Bulgaria	Sept & Jan	9 & 12 months	Adults	800-1,200 BGN	800-1,200 BGN	600-900 $ USD	600-900 $ USD	900-1,350 $ USD	Self-pay, Housing advice provided by employer	No	Tourist Visa, convert to work visa or EU Citizenship	BA and No BA	Phone, email in advance or face-to-face in destination country
Czech Republic	Sept & Jan	10 & 12 months	Adults	15,000-20,000 CZK	15,000-20,000 CZK	870-1,160 $ USD	870-1,160 $ USD	1,300-1,700 $ USD	Self-pay, Housing advice provided by employer	No	Tourist Visa, convert to work visa or EU Citizenship	BA required	Phone, email in advance or face-to-face in destination country
France	Sept & Jan	10 & 12 months	Adults	1,600-2,000 Euro	1,600-2,000 Euro	2,400-3,000 $ USD	2,400-3,000 $ USD	3,600-4,500 $ USD	Self-pay, Housing advice provided by employer	No	Tourist Visa, EU Citizenship	BA required	Face-to-face in destination country
Germany	Sept & Jan	10 & 12 months	Adults	1,600-2,000 Euro	1,600-2,000 Euro	2,400-3,000 $ USD	2,400-3,000 $ USD	3,600-6,000 $ USD	Self-pay, Housing advice provided by employer	No	Tourist Visa, convert to work visa or EU Citizenship	BA required	Face-to-face in destination country
Greece	Sept & Jan	10 & 12 months	Adults	800-1,000 Euro	800-1,000 Euro	1,200-1,500 $ USD	1,200-1,500 $ USD	1,800-2,250 $ USD	Self-pay, Housing advice provided by employer	No	Tourist Visa, EU Citizenship	BA required	Face-to-face in destination country
Hungary	Sept & Jan	10 & 12 months	Adults	150,000 - 200,000 HUF	150,000 - 200,000 HUF	800-1100 $ USD	800-1100 $ USD	1,200-1,650 $ USD	Self-pay, Housing advice provided by employer	No	Tourist Visa, convert to work visa or EU Citizenship	BA required	Face-to-face in destination country
Italy	Sept, Oct & Jan	10 & 12 months	Adults	1,200-1,400 Euro	1,200-1,400 Euro	1,800-2,100 $ USD	1,800-2,100 $ USD	2,700-3,150 $ USD	Self-pay, Housing advice provided by employer	No	Tourist Visa, EU Citizenship	BA required	Face-to-face in destination country
Poland	Sept, Oct & Jan	9 & 12 months	Adults	2,500-2,800 PLN	2,500-2,800 PLN	900-1,000 $ USD	900-1,000 $ USD	1,350-1,500 $ USD	Self-pay, Housing advice provided by employer	No	Tourist Visa, EU Citizenship	BA required in most	Face-to-face in destination country
Portugal	Sept & Jan	10 & 12 months	Adults	1,100-1,400 Euro	1,100-1,400 Euro	1,600-2,100 $ USD	1,600-2,100 $ USD	2,400-3,150 $ USD	Self-pay, Housing advice provided by employer	No	Tourist Visa, EU Citizenship	BA required	Face-to-face in destination country

Europe

Country	Peak Hiring Seasons	Typical Contract Length	Typical Students	Average Monthly Cost of Living in Local Currency	Average Monthly Salary in Local Currency	Average Monthly Cost of Living in $ USD	Average Monthly Salary in $ USD	Approximate Start-up Costs *	Housing	Reimbursed Airfare	Visa Info	Degree Requirement	Interview Procedures
Romania	Sept & Jan	9 & 12 months	Adults	1,100-1,400 RON	1,100-1,400 RON	400-500 $ USD	400-500 $ USD	600-750 $ USD	Self-pay, Housing advice provided by employer	No	Tourist Visa, convert to work visa or EU Citizenship	BA and No BA	Most face-to-face in destination country; Some phone and email in advance
Russia	Sept & Jan	6, 9 & 12 months	Adults	18,500-25,000 RUB	18,500-25,000 RUB	800-1,100 $ USD	800-1,100 $ USD	1,200-1,650 $ USD	Some Free Housing	No/Some return flight	Work visa	BA and No BA	Phone, email in advance or face-to-face in destination country
Slovakia	Sept & Jan	6 & 12 months	Adults	13,000-20,000 SKK	13,000-20,000 SKK	650-1,000 $ USD	650-1,000 $ USD	1,000-1,500 $ USD	Self-pay, Housing advice provided by employer	No	Tourist Visa, convert to work visa or EU Citizenship	BA and No BA	Phone, email in advance or face-to-face in destination country
Spain	Sept, Oct & Jan	10 & 12 months	Adults	1,200-1,500 Euro	1,200-1,500 Euro	1,800-2,200 $ USD	1,800-2,200 $ USD	2,400-3,150 $ USD	Self-pay, Housing advice provided by employer	No	Tourist Visa, EU Citizenship	No BA required	Face-to-face in destination country
Turkey	Year-round	6 & 12 months	Adults	1,000-1,700 TRY	1,000-1,700 TRY	700-1,100 $ USD	700-1,100 $ USD	1,050-1,650 $ USD	Self-pay, Housing advice provided by employer	No	Work visa	BA required	Phone, email in advance or face-to-face in destination country

1) ***Estimated start up costs: based on 1 month average expenses if job is arranged in advance and start working immediately; 1.5 months if arriving in country to interview. Teachers typically receive their pay one time a month. Flight costs are extra expenses to add.**

2) **Costs and wages converted from local currency to US Dollars ($ USD) from worldwide exchange rates at time of printing. Use www.xe.com for current rates. This is a guide only, not exact information.**

3) **Most English teaching jobs listed are for the private language institutes. Public Schools Additional hiring date: China, South Korea, Japan, Taiwan have public school hiring dates in Feb/March and Aug/Sept. Chile public schools start in March.**

Disclaimer: With respect to the information contained in this document, neither TEFL Institute, its agents, contractors nor any of their employees, makes any warranty, express or implied, including the warranties of merchantability and fitness for a particular purpose, or assumes any legal liability or responsibility for the accuracy, completeness, or usefulness of any information provided in this chart. The information is provided only as a guide.

Job Search Process

II. TEFL BASIC, TEFL SEMINAR, AND OTHER COURSES (SELF-PLACEMENT PROCESS)
It is best to plan at least 120 days for your job search. Most of your job search will be conducted online as you visit the various internet job board sites featuring English teaching jobs abroad.

EMAIL THESE DOCUMENTS TO YOUR SCHOOL ONLY

Cover Letter

Cover Letter includes:

- When you expect to depart for your country
- How long you would like to live and teach there
- When do you expect to leave
- Any pertinent information regarding you. Some examples would be:
    - If you are married and traveling with your spouse and children
    - If you are traveling with a pet
    - If you have a disability such as blindness or require the use of a wheelchair
    - Specific skills you may have such as business, medical, or legal experience that would improve your value to work with corporate clients

International Resume

Please review the chapter in this guide on International Resumes for examples and detailed instructions on how to prepare an International Resume.

Photos

You will need to submit to your school two (2) photos:

- Head Shot
- Body Shot

Statement of Purpose

Please prepare a Statement of Purpose using 250 words or less. In this statement be clear about:

- Your commitment to teaching English abroad. Reference your TEFL Certificate as proof.
- Your interest in the culture, language, and customs of the country and desire to make new friends and associates.
- The length of time you are prepared to stay. If you are applying for a 12 month job, you will want to say that you plan to remain for a year or longer in the country.

EMAIL THESE DOCUMENTS TO YOUR SCHOOL ONLY

Job Search Process

TEFL INSTITUTE PROVIDES:

Documents Provided by TEFL Institute

√ TEFL Certificate – mailed to you within 60 days after you complete your TEFL Training Course

√ Letter of Reference

√ Placement Guidebook

You must be prepared to send out many email messages to reach your school. For some it may take as many as 125 inquiries before you find your idea position.

It is best to keep a detailed journal or log with the school names, contact information and date of contact. You can use this log to follow up with your schools and send them any additional information they request.

Job Search Process

JOB SEARCH JOURNAL
TEFL INSTITUTE

Date	School Name	Website	Contact Name	Email	Telephone Number	Item Sent	Follow Up 1	Follow Up 2	Follow Up 3

Job Search Process

III. ROOSEVELT UNIVERSITY STUDENTS

Students taking our TEFL Courses through the Roosevelt University system must have taken and completed at least one of the TEFL courses below:

TESA 101 – Teaching English for Volunteer Teaching 1 – 2 credit hours

TESA 102 – Teaching English for Volunteer Teaching 2 – 1 credit hour

(live in-person course)

TESA 201 – Teaching English as Study Abroad 1 – 2 credit hours

TESA 202 – Teaching English as Study Abroad 2 – 2 credit hours

TESA 203 – Teaching English as Study Abroad 3 (TEFL Practicum) – 0 credit hours

Your placement process will take a minimum of 90 days to complete. It can only be conducted once you have completed your course requirements as prescribed by Roosevelt University. Upon completion of your courses we ask that you follow the process outlined on the next page.

Job Search Process

PROCEDURE FOR PLACEMENT ASSISTANCE:

If you wish the TEFL Institute to assist in job placement in one of the countries listed in the table on page 32, you must follow these procedures:

Steps	Your Action Steps
1	Complete your coursework as required by Roosevelt University.
2	Contact us only after you have completed your coursework, we will need a minimum of 90 days to complete your placement.
3	Contact us at least 3 months prior to your intended start date. *If you are going to teach in Chile, China, Korea, Japan, Taiwan or Vietnam email your resume and photos to TEFL Institute.* If you are not teaching in these countries email your materials to your school.
4	If you email us documents we will forward your resume and photos to the school or recruiter via email.
5	Typically, the recruiter or school will contact you via email.
6	You will set up a phone interview and discuss the details directly with the school or recruiter and not with TEFL Institute.
7	Please ask all of the questions you need be answered in order to feel comfortable and confident before accepting a job.
8	If you both agree to accept the job it is your responsibility to follow through with all the paperwork and arrangements necessary for the work, visa, or hiring agreement terms.
9	You will forward all required documentation directly to the hiring school and work out all housing, salary, and benefit details directly with the school, not with the TEFL Institute.

Job Search Process

DOCUMENTS NEEDED FROM YOU (ACCEPTED BY EMAIL ONLY):

Cover Letter

Cover Letter includes:

- When you expect to depart for your country
- How long you would like to live and teach there
- When do you expect to leave
- Any pertinent information regarding you. Some examples would be:
    - If you are married and traveling with your spouse and children
    - If you are traveling with a pet
    - If you have a disability such as blindness or require the use of a wheelchair
    - Specific skills you may have such as business, medical, or legal experience that would improve your value to work with corporate clients

International Resume

Please review the chapter in this guide on International Resumes for examples and detailed instructions on how to prepare an International Resume.

Photos

You will need to submit to your school two (2) photos:

- Head Shot
- Body Shot

Statement of Purpose

Please prepare a Statement of Purpose using 250 words or less. In this statement be clear about:

- Your commitment to teaching English abroad. Reference your TEFL Certificate as proof.
- Your interest in the culture, language, and customs of the country and desire to make new friends and associates.
- The length of time you are prepared to stay. If you are applying for a 12 month job, you will want to say that you plan to remain for a year or longer in the country.

DOCUMENTS CAN BE ACCEPTED BY EMAIL ONLY

Job Search Process

PLACEMENT COUNTRIES TABLE*

	Countries			
TEFL Institute	Chile Taiwan	China Vietnam	Japan	Korea
Summer Only	Chile	China	Spain	
Volunteer Only	Chile Nepal	Ghana Tanzania	India	Kenya
TEFL Institute School Contacts Available	Costa Rica Indonesia Russia	Estonia Mexico Spain[3]	Germany Peru Turkey	Honduras Poland Uruguay
Use the Guidebook	All Countries			

*The countries listed on this table are subject to change please contact TEFL Institute for the most current list of placement countries.

Teachers must be able to pass any required background, criminal, or educational screenings that is required by their future employer or host organization.

TEFL INSTITUTE

Job Search Process

TEFL INSTITUTE SCHOOL CONTACTS

TEFL Institute conducts a thorough screen of each partner school. It includes a survey with over 50 questions along with requests for photos and testimonials. Every step is taken to help insure TEFL course graduates are placed at highly reputable schools and organizations. Candidates are given contacts at the school and you are to email your cover letter, resume, photo, and statement of purpose directly to that school.

GUIDELINES FOR PLACEMENT ASSISTANCE

To obtain our help you must meet the eligibility requirements for that country. If not, we will ask you to consider another country where we can help you obtain an English teaching job.

TIMELINES AND DUE DATES

We need a minimum of 90 days to conduct your job search. Unfortunately, if you request an earlier departure date or cannot give us enough time conduct your job search, you must conduct a self-placement.

TEFL INSTITUTE CONTACTS

Please note that any and all contacts provided to you by TEFL Institute during this job placement process have undergone an extensive review process. We believe them to be highly reliable and dependable. Many of the recruiters and agents have been with us since our inception.

Some will simply hire you based on our recommendation although we discourage such practices. This is because our previous graduates are outstanding, dedicated, and committed teachers. They have taught at an outstanding level and because they fulfill the duties as well as the duration of their contracts.

We ask that you make every effort to return their email messages and telephone calls in a timely fashion.

Once we have turned you over to a contact. All future contacts will be made between you and the school, recruiter or agent and not TEFL Institute. TEFL Institute does not negotiate school contracts, set up air flights, housing or other matters.

Job Search Process

OUR PLEDGE TO YOU

Our pledge to you, if you are dissatisfied with your placement school, TEFL Institute will help you find a new school. In addition, we will explain to your school why you are leaving to give them an opportunity for improvement (if needed).

TEACHER PAY

As a teacher you will be paid at the local prevailing wage rate in that county. Please see the tables on pages 22-25 for more information on salaries and the best time to find a English teaching abroad.

Materials Checklist

MATERIALS CHECKLIST

At a minimum you will need these documents to apply for an English Teaching job abroad.

Cover Letter

Cover Letter includes:

- When you expect to depart for your country
- How long you would like to live and teach there
- When do you expect to leave
- Any pertinent information regarding you. Some examples would be:
    - If you are married and traveling with your spouse and children
    - If you are traveling with a pet
    - If you have a disability such as blindness or require the use of a wheelchair
    - Specific skills you may have such as business, medical, or legal experience that would improve your value to work with corporate clients

International Resume

Please review the chapter in this guide on International Resumes for examples and detailed instructions on how to prepare an International Resume.

Photos

You will need to submit to your school two (2) photos:

- Head Shot
- Body Shot

Statement of Purpose

Please prepare a Statement of Purpose using 250 words or less. In this statement be clear about:

- Your commitment to teaching English abroad. Reference your TEFL Certificate as proof.
- Your interest in the culture, language, and customs of the country and desire to make new friends and associates.
- The length of time you are prepared to stay. If you are applying for a 12 month job, you will want to say that you plan to remain for a year or longer in the country.

DOCUMENTS CAN BE ACCEPTED BY EMAIL ONLY

Materials Checklist

YOUR SCHOOL MAY REQUEST SOME ADDITIONAL MATERIALS (PLEASE SEE THE POSSIBLE LIST BELOW).

PLEASE DO NOT SEND ANY OF THESE MATERIALS TO TEFL INSTITUTE. YOU WILL SEND THESE MATERIALS TO YOUR SCHOOL ONLY.

Passport Photo-Date Page
Submit a black and white copy of your passport photo-date page to your school. Your Passport must have 2 years remaining on it.

College Transcript and/or College Diploma
Most schools will request official sealed transcripts and/or an official college diploma. If you do not have or want to supply your college diploma, a copy from your college plus a notarization from the consulate of the country you are going to will be required.

References
Ask a former employer, college professor or someone to write a letter on your behalf. The letter should describe your personal attributes on being dependable and your sincere interest to learn more about the country you are visiting.

Medical Form
Some schools will require a physical exam. If your school requires such a form, the school will send you a form to have your doctor complete.

Criminal Background Check
Some schools may require a local and/or state background check. Usually your local police station can conduct such a check. There may be a small one time fee (usually less than a $100). Always check for the official government seals on the letter once you receive it.

International Insurance
Most schools do not provide a comprehensive medical, life, dental, or vision insurance plan to those teaching English abroad. Again, they do NOT provide medical insurance. It is important that you have proper insurance before leaving your home country that will cover you abroad. If you are covered on a family policy held by your parent or guardian, check with the insurance carrier to make sure that your coverage will continue while you are on the program and/or out of the country. Also, if you will reach the age of 21 before or during the program, be certain that your coverage will continue beyond that date. Your insurance should provide trip insurance for flight cancellation. You are free to select the insurance provider of your choice.

Completing Your TEFL Training

Many schools around the world require their teachers to complete a minimum of 100 hours of TEFL training or the equivalent. We have included the syllabus from our TEFL Professional course in this guidebook as a reference tool for you and your school. If your school requests a copy of your course syllabus please feel free to use the syllabus below or to request a copy from TEFL Institute.

TEFL COURSE SYLLABUS
EXAMPLE FROM TEFL PROFESSIONAL COURSE

Class meets: Daily

Required materials:

■ Email address

■ TEFL Institute Online account provided by TEFL Institute

■ A Word Processing Program

Participation and Attendance: You may submit assignments and replies at any time day or night. Email your instructor if you have any questions, or post a message to the Instructors Office of the discussion board.

Assignments and quizzes are the major thrust of the course and due to the intensive schedule; **assignments must be completed on time**. If you fall behind, it will be hard to catch up. **Therefore, you must log in at least once a day to submit assignments, communicate with classmates through online discussions, and take quizzes.**

Course Overview: This course is designed to provide you with quality course work and experiences which will aid you in developing an awareness and mastering teaching skills for the EFL/ESL classroom.

Course Objectives:
In this course you will:

- Develop an awareness of the field and practices of TEFL.
- Develop an understanding of the components of the English Language as related to teaching English to non-native speakers.
- Design lessons for EFL/ESL students at a variety of levels.

Completing Your TEFL Training

- Develop appropriate lesson plans for your English Language Learners in Listening, Speaking, Reading, and Writing.
- Consider and comment on the work of fellow classmates.

Certificate Requirements:

In order to receive your certificate, you will need to:

- Complete all Assignments, Quizzes, Final Exam, and Final Project
- Maintain a 70% overall average
- Complete TEFL Practicum comprised of 20 hours of observation in an EFL/ESL facility with documentation
- Submit via fax or mail the Practicum Time Log and Evaluation Form signed by the cooperating teacher

Final Grades:

A	400-360 points
B	359-320 points
C	319-280 points
Unsatisfactory	279-0 points

Note: All grades will be posted online as soon as the assignments have been graded.

Assignments (400 points):

- Written Assignments 150 points
- Quizzes 170 points
- Final project 50 points
- Final Exam 30 points
- Testimonial (Extra Credit) 5 points

Written Assignments TEFL Institute Online Discussion Board:

For each Written Assignment, you will read the assignment in **Course Material** as you complete the module, or in the Assignments Area. Complete the assignment and submit to the Discussion Board Forum for the assignment. It is wise to first write your assignment in a word processing program, then copy and paste to the discussion board.

Discussion Board Instructions are available in the **Course Information** Area.

Completing Your TEFL Training

Finally you will read ALL the other students' essays on the topic and offer encouragement and suggestions for essay improvements to two of your classmates. You will get instructions with each assignment. *You must log into the course daily, or it will be extremely difficult to keep up. Failure to complete the course on time may delay your placement in an English Teaching Project.*

Completing Your TEFL Training

	Topics	Assignments
Module One	The Field of TESOL/ELT Learning Styles The Teacher's Role Roles and Qualities The Classroom: The Physical Environment	**M1A1** – Learning Styles Discussion Question **Due Day April 25** **M1A2** – My Teachers Discussion Question **Due Day April 27** **M1A3** – Classroom Seating Arrangements Discussion Question **Due Day 6** **M1– Mini Quiz One** **Due Day April 29**
Module Two	History of Language Teaching The "Designer" Approaches of the 1970s and Beyond Communicative Competence and The Post Methods Era The Psychological Learning Environment	**M2A1** – Approaches in ESL/EFL: Discussion Question **Due Day May 3** **M2A2** – Error Correction Discussion Question **Due Day May5** **M2 Mini Quiz One** – Approaches to English Teaching Quiz **M2 Mini Quiz Two** – The Designer Approaches of the 1970's and Beyond **M2 Mini Quiz Three** – Psychological Learning Environments

Completing Your TEFL Training

	Topics	Assignments
Module Three	Students' Needs Principles of Learning a Language A Framework For TEFLPPP Lesson Plans Classroom Strategies STT/TTT and Giving Directions	**M3A1**– Body Parts Discussion Question **Due Day May 11** **M3A2** – Simplifying Teacher Language Discussion Question **Due Day May 13** **M3 – Mini Quiz One** Student Needs **M3 – Mini Quiz Two** Classroom Strategies
Module Four	Teaching Listening Developing and Conducting Speaking Practice Teaching Vocabulary Open Class or Small Group Activities Pronunciation-Intonation Minimal Pairs	**M4A1** – Teaching Listening Discussion Question **Due Day May 17** **M4A2** – Teaching Conversation Discussion Question **Due Day May 19** **M4 – Mini Quiz One** Principles of Teaching Listening **M4 – Mini Quiz Two** Conducting Speaking Practice **M4 – Mini Quiz Three** Pronunciation

Completing Your TEFL Training

	Topics	Assignments
Module Five	Five Reading Strategies Developing Writing Skills Writing Systems Different Languages Providing Written Feedback Writing Lesson Ideas: Patterned Poetry History of English	**M5A1** – Reading Lesson Plan **Due Day May 25** **M5A2** – Writing Lesson Plan **Due Day May 27** **M5 Mini Quiz One** – Teaching Reading **M5 Mini Quiz Two** – Teaching Writing
Module Six	English Structure and Grammar as Compared to Other Languages The Teaching of Grammar English Grammar Review	**M6A1** – Teaching Grammar **Due Day June 2** **M6A2** – The Role of Grammar in the EFL Classroom **Due Day June 4** **M6 Mini Quiz One** – Word Order/Parts of Speech/General Grammar **M6 Mini Quiz Two** – The Twelve Main Verb Tenses **M6 Mini Quiz Three** – Phrasal Verbs and MultiWord Verbs **M6 Mini Quiz Four** – Reported Speech **M6 Mini Quiz Five** – The Conditionals **M6 Mini Quiz Six** – Passive Voice

Completing Your TEFL Training

	Topics	Assignments
Module Seven	Seven Visuals ESL Textbooks and Supplemental Materials Online Resources, Video, and CALL (Computer Assisted Language Learning) Games for the Classroom Assessing Student Performance Standardized Tests for English Students	**M7A1–** Resources Web Quest **Due Day June 8** **M7A2** – Design an Assessment **Due Day June 10** **M7 Mini Quiz One** – Visuals, Games, and Resources **M7 Mini Quiz Two–** Assessment
Module Eight	1. Formal Lesson Planning 2. The Cover Page 3. The Procedure Section 4. Thematic Unit Final Project	**M8** – Final Project: Thematic Unit Due Day June 19 **M8 – Final Exam** Due Day June 22
Module Nine	1. Final Project Review 2. Preparing for Culture Shock 3. Professional Development	**M9A1**– Course Reflection **Due Day June 22**

Completing Your TEFL Training

We are very proud of our practicum training sessions. It provides an opportunity for students to apply the methods, approaches and theories learned at TEFL Institute to an actual ESL/EFL classroom with supervised teaching. The practicum begins after you have completed all of the necessary written coursework and assignments.

You will volunteer (not-for-pay) as a tutor or English teaching assistant with a local ESL Institute in your community. In most cities in the United Kingdom or North America, you can find a local ESL institute by checking with community based organizations serving non-native English speakers, government agencies or professional English language institutes. The certificate requires all students to complete at least 20 hours of practicum experience (for students in the Basic course, the practicum is only recommended and not required because that course is only an introductory level course).

Candidates participating in the practicum experience can learn the practical aspects of class lesson planning with clear teaching objectives, predicting learner outcomes, leveraging various kinds of methodologies and using assessment tools to motivate and reward students. Observation and feedback sessions with the instructor are highly encouraged and expected as a part of your certification process.

We believe the practicum experience is vital to becoming a well versed ESL instructor before you begin teaching abroad because:

- The students you will be teaching are real ESL students with real needs and typical language concerns. The TEFL Institute has been working closely with nonprofit agencies in Chicago to help adult learners from African, Eastern European and South American countries with their language skills as they move into Chicago and the surrounding communities. You will be their teacher, tutor, mentor or advisor. They are there to learn and are extremely eager to advance in English.

Completing Your TEFL Training

The relationship between you and the students will be rewarding for each of you. They learn English from you and you learn how to be a teacher from them. Everyone wins!

- Your teaching schedule is designed to mirror as closely as possible the experience of working in an authentic fast paced language school. For this reason, you will be doing lots of tutoring, teaching or whatever it takes to help your students learn English! Your students may be at the beginning, intermediate, or advanced levels of English Language communication. They are there to become more proficient in order to help them gain a job or just to communicate clearly with new friends and family in the area. Again we feel this is the only way to be fully prepared for those first hectic months in a new ESL job abroad.

- The TEFL Institute will assist each successful graduate in finding a volunteer or paid English teaching project abroad.

TEFL CHICAGO PRACTICUM

This is a great way to not only get some authentic teaching experience under your belt (and onto your resume!) but also a great way to give back to the community.

The minimum time commitment is 20 volunteer hours over four weeks. You will need to be prompt, enthusiastic, and dependable. At the end of this session, your supervisor will complete an evaluation of your performance.

Upon successful completion of your practicum experience, you will be awarded your TEFL certification.

INTERNATIONAL PRACTICUM

The practicum at our international locations will be coordinated by the school director. You will work 20 hours as a volunteer instructor, tutor or observer at a local ESL School before beginning your paid or volunteer teaching assignment.

PRACTICUM LOG

In order to complete the requirements for the TEFL Certificate, you must complete 20 hours of observation/practicum time. This practicum will be in an ESL or EFL classroom of your choice.

Completing Your TEFL Training

PRACTICUM TIME LOG

Write the dates, times and total hours for each session of observation or volunteer teaching. Then you will need to mail or fax the completed form with the name of the facility at which you observed, the signature of the cooperating teacher, and their email for confirmation of your hours.

- In order to receive your TEFL Certificate, the Time Log must be submitted to TEFL Institute along with the TEFL Evaluation Form.
- If you are working with more than one teacher you are required to submit a time log for each teacher you work with.
- If you are working in more than one school you are required to submit a time log for each location.

Date	Time	Total Hours

TEFL Student: ______________________________ Date: ____________

Cooperating Teacher: __________________________ Date: ____________

Email: ____

Name of Cooperating Program:

____

Address: ____

Please fax or email this form along with the TEFL Evaluation to:

TEFL Institute

1906 W. Irving Park Road

Chicago, IL 60613

Fax: (773) 880-5940

Email: studentservices@teflinstitute.com

Completing Your TEFL Training

TEFL EVALUATION FORM

(Type or print clearly)
Participant's Name:

____

Prefix (Mr./Ms./Dr.) Last Name (Family Name) First Middle

Institution Name and Address:

____

City, State/Province, Postal Code, Country

Phone: ______________________ Email Address: ______________________

Country: ______________ Website Address for School: ______________________

In accordance with the TEFL Board recommendations, TEFL INSTITUTE requires participants to complete at least 20 hours of practicum training with their assigned school before starting their teaching assignment. Please offer your evaluation of the Participant's progress during training and teaching at your school. Participants must gain a satisfactory or above rating in every category in order to receive their full TEFL Certification from TEFL INSTITUTE.

EVALUATION BY:

Name: ______________________ Address: ______________________

Title: ______________________ Phone: ______________________

Institution: ______________________ Email Address: ______________________

Capacity in which you train the applicant: ______________________

The TEFL Institute Programs may call me about my recommendation: ____ Yes ____ No

The TEFL Certification abroad experience calls for maturity, responsibility, flexibility and sensibility. Your honest evaluation will be most helpful to us and to the English Teacher. Thank you for your cooperation.

Please use the list below to give a general profile of the applicant.

MOTIVATION	Excellent	Good	Satisfactory	Needs Work	Unsatisfactory
Seriousness of Purpose	______	______	______	______	______
Interest in ESL Teaching	______	______	______	______	______
Intellectual Curiosity	______	______	______	______	______
Desire to teach others	______	______	______	______	______

TEFL EVALUATION FORM

PAGE 2

Participant's Name: ______________________________

RESPONSIBILITY	Excellent	Good	Satisfactory	Needs Work	Unsatisfactory
Completes work					
Arrives on time					
Takes directions well					
Handles stress well					

RELATING TO OTHERS	Excellent	Good	Satisfactory	Needs Work	Unsatisfactory
Sensitivity to diversity					
Nonjudgmental					
Caring, kind, & friendly					
Works well with others					
Adjusts to new areas					

TEACHING ABILITIES	Excellent	Good	Satisfactory	Needs Work	Unsatisfactory
Class Lesson Planning					
Knowledge of Grammar					
Presentation Skills					
Teaching Methodology					
Teaching Enthusiasm					

Additional Comments that you feel would be helpful in evaluating this applicant:

____

____

____

SUMMARY

- ❑ I RECOMMEND FOR TEFL CERTIFICATION WITHOUT RESERVATION
- ❑ I HAVE SOME DOUBTS, BUT STILL RECOMMEND
- ❑ I HAVE DOUBTS AND ADVISE YOU TO SEEK ADDITIONAL INFORMATION
- ❑ I DO NOT BELIEVE THE APPLICANT IS WELL-SUITED FOR ENGLISH TEACHING

______________________________ ____________

Signature Date

Completing Your TEFL Training

TEFL CERTIFICATE

It is important to keep a copy of your TEFL "Certificate of Completion" on file and to submit it to your school along with:

- International Resume
- Photo
- Statement of Purpose
- TEFL Reference Letter

The TEFL Certificate verifies your completion of TEFL training and can qualify you for higher wages with your school. Many schools will pay you 20% to 40% more each month because you have completed a TEFL training program or the equivalent. Your TEFL Certificate should include the number of hours completed in your TEFL training along with any organizations that recognize your institute as a TEFL provider.

Standard Certificate Package – Certificate with Letter of Recommendation provided at no extra charge.

Deluxe Certificate Package – Certificate with Letter of Recommendation and Certificate Holder (Certificate holders available at an additional cost. Please contact TEFL Institute's Student Services Department for pricing.)

A duplicate copy of your TEFL Certificate can be ordered through Students Services for an additional fee. Please contact TEFL Institute's Student Services Department at studentservices@teflinstitute.com.

Completing Your TEFL Training

REFERENCE LETTER FROM TEFL INSTITUTE

Below is a sample reference letter that TEFL Institute will provide to you for your school. TEFL Institute is happy to provide references for any successful graduate of our courses.

Sample Reference Letter

May 2010

Dear School Director:

TEFL Institute is pleased to recommend John Smith as an English Language instructor for your institution.

TEFL Institute is a recognized member of the Illinois Teachers of ESOL & Bilingual Education, California TESOL Instructors of America, Accreditation Council for TESOL Distance Learning Education Courses, International Association of Teaching English as a Foreign Language, Association of International Educators, The College of Teachers, Open Distance Learning and Quality Council, and The TEFL Board.

The US State Department's Fulbright Program recommends TEFL Institute as an internationally recognized TEFL Certification Course provider.

Our courses are recognized and approved by the Illinois State Board of Education for up to 60 CEU/CPDU teacher certification credits.

TEFL Institute offers weekend, in-person, and online courses. We offer TEFL Programs in over 17 countries around the world through our affiliated partners. Please feel free to contact our office for additional information on this instructor.

Sincerely,

Ti Ron Gibbs

Ti Ron Gibbs
President
TEFL Institute

1906 W. Irving Park Road • Chicago, IL 60613 • main: (773) 880-5141 • fax: (773) 880-5940 • **www.teflinstitute.com**

International Resume Guide

WHAT IS AN INTERNATIONAL RESUME?

An international resume is very similar to a regular resume or CV except that it includes personal information about you. In the United States much of this information would never be included on a resume and it is probably against the law for the US companies to request such information.

However, when you are going abroad, schools and organizations do not have to follow the code of conduct and laws of the United States or your home country.
Our experience has shown that most schools are not trying to disqualify candidates based on their race, ethnicity, or other factors. Rather, they are typically trying to insure that housing and related matters are in order for arrival in case they decided to hire you.

International Resume Guide

International Resume Writing Guide

by Ti Ron Gibbs
President and Founder
TEFL Institute

TEFL Institute is happy to provide this guide to those who are interested in teaching English abroad. When writing an International Resume it is important to remember that most of the time your education and academic pursuits are given more attention than your actual work experience. List your education, skills, certification, and course work in a clear and concise manner. And, always include your country code in your contact telephone number.

Formatting Your Resume

1. Open Microsoft Word Page Setup

- Set the page margins to 1" (2.54 cm) all around (top, bottom, left, and right)
- Set your default font to Times New Roman or Arial
- Set your font size to 10 or 12 point
- Justify all text alignments to the left

2. Save your resume under a name such as: "John Smith Resume.doc"
3. Center your contact information at the top of the page:

John Smith
johnsmith@teflinstitute.com
0017735555555
New Haven, Connecticut – United States of America

4. Do not use bold, italics, or other font enhancements as your write your resume.
5. Never abbreviate terms such as "Mgr." or "V.P." Use "Manager" or "Vice President" instead.
6. Use universal position titles. Try "Receptionist" and not "Telephone Operator."
7. Now you are ready to start writing your resume. Most of your information will come under these five sections:

International Resume Guide

a. **PERSONAL INFORMATION** – list information on gender, age, and marital status.

b. **EDUCATION** – include any and all programs, degrees, certifications, and other formalized training programs that you attended in-person or online.

c. **SKILLS** – summarize your skills in computers, animation, sales, and any other areas.

d. **CAREER EXPERIENCE** – be prepared to list your company, job title, and dates of employment for the past 10 years. Foreign companies and institutions are very interested in job titles. Try to find a way to equate your title with something that anyone can understand. For instance, your title may be "Recruiter" at your current job but use the term "Human Resources Specialist/Manager" instead.

e. **EXTRACURRICULAR INTEREST** –list the things you like to do in your spare time. Many companies want to make sure that when you come to a country you are outgoing, independent, and can find your own way. List your swimming awards, an article wrote, or a photography class contest you entered.

- Bear in mind that every country is unique and they seek individuals who bring additional skills that are not available in the local talent pool. Your resume should reflect your unique strengths, skills, and experiences. Mention that you are a "native English speaker."
- Look at the requirements of the position and make sure that you show clearly how you meet all, or as many as possible, of the criteria.

SECTION HEADINGS

PERSONAL INFORMATION

You will list pertinent information regarding gender, age, and marital status:

- Include Gender Information (Male, Female, or Other)
- Include Date of Birth, use the international format (12 July 1903)
- Include Nationality (the place your passport is issued)
- List Work Permits held (Chinese Z Visa for six months)
- List Country of Citizenship (the place you have the legal right to vote)

International Resume Guide

EDUCATION

Include any and all programs, degrees, certifications, and other formalized training programs that you attended in-person or online.

■ List your highest-level qualifications first

■ Be specific and detailed about the institution, major, campus location, date of completion of final degrees listed

■ If you are applying for an ESL Teaching assignment and do not have an Education Degree, list your college classes in that area (English Literature, Journalism in India, Public Speaking, Spanish, etc.)

Examples:

The University of Virginia – Charlottesville, Virginia, United States of America, Bachelor of Arts in Political Science, Minor in East Asian Studies, May 1985

The University of Hong Kong – Hong Kong, China, Bachelor of Arts in Business, Bachelor of Arts in Finance, Minor in Chinese, August 1999

Relevant Coursework Includes: English Literature, Western Thought, Democracy Theory, etc.

SKILLS

Summarize your skills in computers, animation, sales, and any other areas in one word bullet points.

■ List the skills that you can perform proficiently

■ Back up your skills with experience summaries or interests

■ List any projects you worked upon (volunteer or otherwise)

Example:

Dreamweaver, CGI Pearl, Adobe, Quark and Flash Programmer – Designed 20 page website for "Martha's X and Y House." Informed and recruited volunteers, donors, and workers in the center's mission to fight the spread of AIDS in South Africa.

International Resume Guide

CAREER EXPERIENCE

Be prepared to list your company, job title, and dates of employment for the past 10 years. Foreign companies and institutions are very interested in job titles. Try to find a way to equate your title with something that anyone can understand. For instance, your title may be "Recruiter" at your current job but use the term "Human Resources Specialist/Manager" instead.

- List your work experience starting with the most recent or relevant assignment
- First, list your Job Title, use universal career titles, list the start and end dates
- Second, list the Company's name and its headquarters location
- Third, in a few sentences tell a little about what the company does
- Mention any relevant accomplishment or responsibility

Example of Work Experience

Vice President of Business Development, Kemper Consulting Group, London, England, October 2000 – March 2003.

Kemper Consulting Group is an international consulting practice specializing in financial forecasting and corporate acquisition management throughout Europe, Africa, and Southeast Asia.

• Lead a team of 15 conference and event team managers in Hong Kong and China involving successfully attracting, interviewing and following through with representatives of foreign companies for potential mergers and acquisitions with Chinese enterprises.

• Coordinated public and media relations including writing press releases, conducting interviews, media tie-ups, and follow-up.

• Coordinated event marketing including direct marketing, advertising management, networking, database management, writing bimonthly newsletter, website, marketing materials, etc.

Extracurricular Interest

List the things you like to do in your spare time. Many companies want to make sure that when you come to a country you are outgoing, independent, and can find your own way. List your swimming awards, an article wrote, or a photography class contest you entered.

- List activities that you truly enjoy. A good rule of thumb is to pick a few activities that you have participated in for about ten years (off and on).

International Resume Guide

- List awards, trophies, honors, and articles about your activity
- List any offices, board membership, or leadership positions held
- Show your commitment to this activity

References

While they are not mandatory, they are a good addition to the International Resume. There is no need to list your current employer unless you want them contacted. Try to list at least three references that you know well.

- Provide their name, title, company/school name, telephone number (include country code) and email address.

Next Steps

The first step in the international interview is typically a telephone interview. Try to take into account the time and day difference when committing to an interview slot.

- Check the time and date zones before committing to a telephone interview.
- Use a landline or (hard line) for your interview. Do not use a cell phone. Dropped international calls are confusing for both parties.
- Be on time. Do not let your voicemail or answering machine pick up the call.
- Send a picture prior to the telephone interview. This will help the employer gain a better feel for you.
- Don't waffle during the telephone interview. If you have a telephone interview, tell them that you want the job.

After the Telephone Interview

Send a thank you note as a document attachment via email.

- Scan any documents your employer requested and send as an attachment via email. Inform your employer that you are sending the hard copies of your resume and other materials by regular mail.
- Be sure to send two photos. One should be a headshot and the other a body shot. Business attire and a smile are always acceptable.

When possible, send all international correspondence via certified delivery. You want to be sure that your future employer will receive your materials. A delay could cost you the job.

MARY JONES

100 MAIN STREET, PORTLAND, OR 97404
PHONE 00 - 1 - 555 - 222 - 2222 • E-MAIL MARYJONES@HOTMAIL.COM

Native English Speaker
Citizenship : USA
D.O.B. : April 18, 1984
Gender : Female
Marital Status : Single

PROFILE

Recent college graduate who majored in Spanish and minored in Secondary Education. Extensive experience with children both in and out of the classroom. Skills and experience teaching a foreign language and teaching English. Strong desire to share passion for languages, different cultures, and a global mentality as a teacher. Personal interest in expanding knowledge of Spanish and other cultures. International travel experience. Knowledge of French and German as well.

EDUCATION

Bachelor of Arts in Spanish/Minor in Education GPA: 3.84
University of Portland *Graduation: May 2006*

- Granada, Spain Study Abroad Program, Dean's List, Presidential Scholarship, Ford Scholarship, Alpha Lambda Delta Honor Society, French Achievement Award

TRAINING

120 hour TEFL Certification Graduation: Sept 2005
TEFL Institute *Chicago, IL, USA*

TEACHING EXPERIENCE

*contacts can be provided upon request

Preschool Spanish Teacher Oct. 2005-May 2006
First Presbyterian Church Preschool *Vancouver, WA*

- Design and implement weekly lessons for a full school year to 10 three- to five-year-olds in order to give them a foundation in the Spanish language; incorporate a variety of activities and a supplemental video to maintain engagement and provide most effective learning.

Bridge Builders Academic Mentor Sept. 2005-April 2006
University of Portland/Prospective Gents Club *Portland, OR*

- Create, teach, and evaluate weekly lessons and provide tutoring and guidance for a full school year to 5-8 high

African-American boys working towards college matriculation.

After School Program Tutor Feb. 2006-March 2006

Ortiz Center *Portland, OR*

- Work with 10-20 bilingual students from second grade to sixth grade; help them with their homework and organize activities that stimulate one of their multiple intelligences.

English Teacher/Assistant Sept. 2004-Dec. 2004

Rose City Park School *Portland, OR*

- Assisted another teacher in teaching 5-8 migrant parents basic English that was relevant to their life situations; for example, helping them be verbal and independent in parent-teacher conferences (as opposed to completely relying on a translator), helping them carry basic conversations, helping them checkout at a store.

OTHER EXPERIENCE AND ACTIVITIES

Special Education Classroom Assistant	Spring 2005
Tutor/Mentor for disadvantaged 8th grader	2002-2003 school year
Outdoor School Camp Counselor	May 2000-May 2006
Campus Program Board, Major Event Chair	Aug. 2004-May 2006
Club Soccer, Team Captain	May 2003-Oct 2005
Rebuilding Together Volunteer	Spring 2005

RELEVANT COURSEWORK

Intro to Education	Portland, OR
Advanced Spanish Conversation and Composition	Portland, OR
Advanced Spanish Composition and Grammar	Granada, Spain
Spanish Speaking and Writing Skills	Granada, Spain
Islamic Culture in Spain	Granada, Spain
Spanish Culture and Civilization	Granada, Spain
Spanish Art: Ancient and Medieval	Granada, Spain
Literature and Culture of Contemporary Mexico	Portland, OR
Foundations of Education	Portland, OR
Human Development	Portland, OR
Psychology of Learning	Portland, OR
Special Education	Portland, OR
Hispanic Women Writers	Portland, OR
Classroom Management	Portland, OR
Models of Teaching/Literacy Development	Portland, OR

John Jones
100 East Ontario Street, Unit 100
Chicago, IL 60611
001-333-444-555
johnjones@yahoo.com

Age: 50
Birth Date: 22 February, 1956
Nationality: American
Marital Status: Single
Gender: Male
Native-English Speaker: Yes
Other: I am a certified Public School Teacher in Chicago with a Masters in Education from Roosevelt University and TEFL Professional Certification from the TEFL Institute.

OBJECTIVE

To teach English as a foreign language and provide cultural and business perspective based on my extensive and varied professional experiences.

EDUCATION

TEFL Professional Certificate, TEFL Institute, Chicago, IL
Master of Arts, Elementary Education, Roosevelt University, Chicago, IL
Master of Business Administration, Loyola University, Chicago, IL
Bachelor of Science in Finance, DePaul University, Chicago, IL

SUMMARY OF EXPERIENCE

- Cadre substitute teacher in major public school system. State of Illinois Type 03 (Kindergarten-Grade 9) teaching certificate holder.
- Graduate of Master of Arts in Elementary Education and TEFL programs.
- Business executive with extensive experience in private and commercial banking. Skilled in credit administration, financial planning, and developing budgets for banking entities. Highly successful at managing and servicing client relationships.
- Senior non-commissioned officer, U.S. Army Reserves, with proven experience in unit leadership, operations, planning, training, and recruiting.

PROFESSIONAL EXPERIENCE

CHICAGO PUBLIC SCHOOLS
Elizabeth Peabody Elementary, Chicago, IL
Cadre substitute teacher ***(Feb 2006 - June 2006)***
Student teacher, multi-grades 5th and 6th ***(Sep 2005 - Dec 2005)***

THE NORTHERN TRUST COMPANY, Chicago, IL
Wealth Management Group, Personal Financial Services Business Unit (1996 - 2003)
Vice President. Banking Client Services Representative and Business Group Controller
Commercial Banking Business Unit, Financial & Administration Division (1993 - 1995)
Vice President. Senior Business Unit Analyst-Controller
Financial Markets Division - Financial Institutions Group (1986 - 1993)
Vice President. Credit Administrator, Operations Manager, and Group Controller

U.S. ARMY RESERVES (*Retired - July 2001)*

-continued-

HIGHLIGHTS OF PROFESSIONAL ACHIEVEMENTS

RESULTS

- Achieved credit portfolio growth of 350% over five-year period to $1+ billion with equivalent revenue growth as member of 4-person, private banking team servicing ultra-high net worth clientele.
- Successfully integrated the financial reporting and planning system for the strategic merger of the two major institutional client business units within the corporation.
- Brought a new military unit specializing in radio-television broadcasting from the start-up stage to the most mission capable and ready unit of its kind with personnel serving worldwide.
- Fielded the first-of-its-kind, rapidly deployable commercial AM-FM radio and television production studio and transmitter for foreign civil-military operations.

TRAINING

- Teaching - introduced SMART Board™ interactive whiteboard technology into daily content area instruction for 5th and 6th grade levels.
- Business - trained administrative, support, and relationship staff in banking operations.
- Military - qualified instructor with extensive experience in planning and conducting classes and briefings for basic trainee to senior-level officer audiences.

LEADERSHIP

- Responsible for all aspects of leading a high-priority, 71-soldier Army Reserves unit in operations, training, logistics, administrative support, and recruiting.
- Served as Senior Drill Sergeant for basic training units.

DIGITIZING YOUR RESUME DOCUMENTS

Once you have completed writing your international resume, it is time to turn your paper documents into digital media. You can do this with the use of a scanner or by using Adobe PDF software.

If you do not own a scanner or Adobe, visit Kinko's or another similar store. There you can use their scanning equipment or software for your materials and begin saving your resume as needed.

SAVING YOUR RESUME

Naming your documents is an important step. This little step can help insure that your files are not lost or confused with someone else.

a. Save your resume and cover letter as Word files ending in .doc

b. Save any photo or scanned materials as .jpg or .jpeg files

c. Name your files in the following manner: "Lastname, Firstname Kindofdocument.ext."

For a resume: Jones, John Resume.doc
For a cover letter: Jones, John Cover Letter.doc
For a photo: Jones, John Photo. jpg
For a transcript: Jones, John Transcript.jpg
For a diploma: Jones, John Diploma.jpg

Interviews and Contracts

GETTING THE INTERVIEW

Now that you have completed your TEFL training, it is time to "get the interview" with your school abroad. Your TEFL Certificate, cover letter, international resume, and reference letters are all integral tools in this process. In this Chapter, we provide you with an extensive list of questions that we learned over time. As we developed this list, we also came across an article by Jonathan Clark that we think encapsulates them all in the best possible manner.

THE TEFL JOB INTERVIEW
The 10 Most Important Questions to Ask
By Jonathan Clark

If you are a new teacher or even an experienced teacher who hasn't taught in a foreign setting before, there are certain things you need to know in order to gauge the desirability of a TEFL job.

1. How many teaching hours does the position involve?

2. How many preps will I have? In other words, how many different courses will I be teaching? At the very least, you'll spend one hour of preparation time out of class for every hour in class (a 2:1 ratio is probably more likely, especially if you're a new teacher. Two preps is probably the ideal.)

3. How big are the classes?

4. What textbook does the school use? The important thing isn't so much which particular book they use but to make sure there is one. You'll probably end up modifying a lot of textbook lessons and you'll create a lot of your lessons on your own, but it's always good to have a textbook to fall back on.

5. What sorts of audiovisual equipment are available? Having regular access to a good CD and cassette player is essential. Also, ask about video equipment, since you'll probably want to watch videos from time to time. And see if there's a computer lab where you can take or send your students for writing projects, interactive CD-ROM activities, or Internet research.

6. What are the resources for teachers? You will want to know if the school has a library with a good supply of resource books and if there are computers with Internet access available. You'll need to be able to print documents from the computers. Copy machine access is also very important: you'll create a lot of your own materials that you'll need to copy for your students.

7. Who are the students and why are they studying English? Students studying English at high schools or universities are usually doing so to fill a graduation requirement or because it's useful in their major. But language schools attract people from a variety of backgrounds and age groups with a variety of reasons for studying English. Adult professionals often come to language schools looking for business English instruction or other specialized courses. Also, many language schools cater heavily to children and function largely as an afterschool program. If this is the case, keep in mind that kids generally don't sign up for classes after school of their own accord. Motivation and discipline can be issues when teaching kids.

8. What benefits does the school provide their teachers? It's not common but still possible that a school might offer things like medical benefits, paid vacations, and holiday bonuses. Some offer reimbursements for your travel expenses to and from their country. And most schools offer their teachers free classes in the local language and history or fun stuff like cooking and dancing instruction.

9. Does the school provide assistance with housing? Some schools have apartments for their teachers. If they don't, see if they can offer you some assistance in finding a place once you get there. Having a native speaker along to help negotiate can save you from getting ripped off by a greedy landlord.

10. What are the visa requirements for the job? If you're going to teach at a university or a primary or secondary school you'll likely be required to obtain a legal work visa. Find out what role the employer will have in order to help you get the visa and if they'll pay the fees. Do they have a lawyer or university official who handles the paperwork? Immigration officials can be difficult to deal with, especially when there's a language barrier. Be sure to ask about what you'll need to bring with you in order to get the visa. Some countries require that you apply for the visa at their embassy in your home country, so obviously you will need to get that taken care of before leaving.

One final note: If for some reason the pay for the job wasn't included in the announcement or if you're interviewing for an unannounced position, expect it to be brought up by the interviewer. If that doesn't happen and you feel uncomfortable about bringing it up yourself, try a roundabout approach. Start asking questions about local rents, transportation fees, and food prices. This might cue the interviewer to bring up teacher salaries in relation to these figures.

Interviews and Contracts

TEFL INTERVIEWS & CONTRACTS

What questions will I be asked in the TEFL interview?

TEFL interviews, whether by phone or in person, can last anywhere from 10 minutes to an hour or more. Questions can vary considerably, but here are some of the more common types you may be asked. Many of these questions relating to previous teaching may not be relevant if this is your first job, but you could be asked similar questions about the teaching practice from your training course.

Remember that interviewers often look for concrete examples of skills or behaviors. A question such as, "Can you control disruptive students?" is less likely than "Tell me about a time where you had a disruptive student or class and how you successfully dealt with the situation."

Typical Questions an employer may ask in an interview

- What are your strengths and weaknesses?
- What are your interests outside of work?
- Do you speak any foreign languages?
- Tell me about your experiences learning a foreign language.

Questions about your training

What was the most important thing you learned in your training?

- Why do you think you were awarded an A/B/Pass grade?
- Have you attended any additional training or seminars recently?

Questions about your current and previous employment

- Where are you working at the moment?
- What are your responsibilities in your current position?
- What have you learned from this job?
- Tell me about your previous jobs. Why did you leave?
- Why are you looking for a new job?

Questions about the school and country

- What interests you about this school?
- What do you know about this school?
- Why do you want to live in this country?

Interviews and Contracts

Questions about your teaching and experience

- What are your strengths and weaknesses as a teacher?
- How would you introduce the past simple tense to a group of 10 adult students?
- How would you explain "proud"?
- What would you want to know about a group if I told you I needed you to teach it in 30 minutes?
- What ages and levels of students have you taught in the past?
- Have you ever had to teach without materials? How would you feel about this?
- Tell me about your experience teaching children / business English / TOEFL. How would you feel about being asked to teach this type of class?
- What aspects of your teaching have changed with experience?
- How would your approach with a one-to-one student differ to that with a group?
- What course books do you have experience using? What do you think of them?
- Can you think of a time when you've successfully dealt with a difficult student or class?
- How would you deal with a class of students of mixed abilities?
- Tell me about a time when you felt rewarded or satisfied by something you did in a classroom.
- Have you used multimedia (video, DVD, CD-ROM) in the classroom?

Questions about your expectations

- Have you lived or traveled abroad before?
- What cultural differences did you find difficult to get used to?
- Working in this country can be frustrating. The photocopier may break and go unrepaired for a week. Have you had to deal with situations like this before? How do you think you'd deal with them?
- We expect our teachers to be flexible and supportive of colleagues and other staff. Can you think of a time when you've been flexible or supportive?
- How much support do you expect from a school?
- How do you feel about working split shifts and weekends?
- Do you think it is important for the whole school to be an English speaking environment (not just the classrooms)?

Questions about your future

- Where do you want to be in five years?
- How do you see your future in teaching?

Interviews and Contracts

During your TEFL interview, and at any stage before and after, you should be given the opportunity to ask any questions you have.

What questions should I ask?

There are some things which you need to be clear about before signing a contract:

- For example, if the school works on Saturdays and this is a problem for you, or if you want the possibility of overtime but it is not included in the offer, you need this information to decide if the position is for you.
- Are they willing to offer you a job without speaking to you first?
- Are they unprepared to put you in contact with current teachers?
- Are they expecting you to accept a job offer without seeing a contract?
- Are they asking you to send them money? (There should be no reason for this)

Here are some of the questions you may want to ask:

- What are the working days and working hours? (do you mind working Saturdays?)
- How many contact teaching hours will I be expected to do? (20 to 25 a week is common with 12-15 hours of lesson planning. 40 contact hours a week can be common in language schools in Japan but typically no prep time needed.)
- Will I be paid overtime if I teach more than this number of hours? (when is it paid and is it compulsory?)
- What non-teaching tasks am I required to do? (administration, creating materials, marking, placement testing of students)
- How many days of paid holiday are there? (and does this include public holidays?)
- Is there a probationary period where either party can terminate the contract? (a period of up to 3 months is common where either you or the school can end things)
- What is my salary?
- When and how is it paid? Is there an end of contract bonus? (what are the conditions under which this is paid?)

Interviews and Contracts

IF WORKING ABROAD:

- Is medical insurance provided? (particularly important in countries which do not have reciprocal agreements with your own)
- Is my flight ticket paid? (and when?)
- Is accommodation provided? (is it shared, how much does it cost, how far is it from the school, does it have a TV/fridge/bed?)
- Does the school provide local language lessons for teachers?

QUESTIONS TO ASK OF THE SCHOOL'S INSTRUCTORS FROM THE USA

You can of course ask any of the above questions to teachers as well, for a different perspective, as well as some of these:

- What's the atmosphere in the school like?
- What teaching resources are provided?
- How do you get on with the Director of Studies and/or School Director?
- Do you get paid on time?
- Has the school fulfilled their side of the contract?
- Why are you leaving? (if he/she is leaving)
- What's the city nightlife like?
- What's the accommodation like?
- Is there internet access at the school?
- Does the photocopier work?

When entering into a contract it is imperative you be specific in the questions you ask about contractual offers. Here are some helpful questions to ask.

- What type of students will you be teaching?
- What grades will you be teaching?
- What is the class size?
- Where will you be housed?
- Are you responsible for any utilities?
- Is there hot running water?
- Do you have heating/air conditioning?
- How close are you to the school where you'll be teaching?
- Do you have to share your apartment?
- How many rooms does it have?
- Is it on campus?
- Is there a washing machine?
- Ask for a photo of the living arrangements.

- Is there a computer with internet access?
- Do you have to pay for the internet services?
- Do you have to work for a certain time before your employer will reimburse your airfare?
- How many days do you have off for vacations?
- What are the terms of getting a work visa?
- How many hours will you be teaching a week?
- Will you be required to do daily lesson plans?
- Are you required to work in the school office?

CHECK TO SEE IF YOUR SCHOOL HAS ITS OWN CURRICULUM OR WILL YOU NEED TO WRITE IT.

- What is the curriculum?
- Is it a set curriculum? If so, look at the texts and make sure they aren't antiquated, boring and inappropriate for teaching English.
- Are you supposed to develop any part of the curriculum?

WHAT HAPPENS AFTER THE INTERVIEW?

The school may check your references, and possibly even do a second interview. If everything has gone well, they will then offer you a contract. This will usually be for one year.

Read the contract very carefully and don't be afraid to ask if anything is not clear. A reputable employer will appreciate the fact that moving to another country to live and work is a big step (if you are dealing with the Director of Studies, he/she was probably in the same boat once) and should be forthcoming with help.

Get as much information as you can from the school, other teachers, TEFL websites and forums, so that you can feel comfortable before making a decision.

Interviews and Contracts

There is no set format or content of a TEFL contract. However, it should at least be clear about:

1. Working days and working hours (including contact teaching hours)
2. Holidays (how many days?)
3. Probationary Period (if any, and how long?)
4. Start and end dates of the contract
5. Salary and overtime (including when it is paid)
6. Flight reimbursement (if relevant, including when it is paid)
7. Medical insurance (if relevant)
8. Bonus (if any, including when it is paid)

SURVIVING YOUR FIRST FEW WEEKS
The first few weeks in your first TEFL job can be both exciting and terrifying. You're probably in a new country, a different culture, and it's the first time since your TEFL training that you've been thrown in front of a group of students. You will probably start thinking "Why am I here?"

In developing countries, there tends to be a strong network of support from the school and other teachers. Someone will probably meet you at the airport, show you around the area, go with you to the supermarket for the first time, and take you to the police station to stamp forms, all the while dealing with language barriers for you along the way. If the school provides accommodation, you will be able to just walk in the door and unpack, rather than arriving in a city and spending days searching for an apartment. You may also be living with other teachers, often very near to the school, which provides an extra measure of support, as well as a feeling that you are all in this together.

In English speaking countries and most of Western Europe, you will most likely be expected to sort things out for yourself in terms of getting to the country, finding accommodation and sorting out a lot of the paperwork and visa necessities. The type of support network mentioned above is often much less evident.

Interviews and Contracts

THE FIRST WEEKS OF WORK

With luck, you will be eased into a full teaching schedule gradually, and given plenty of support from other teachers and your Director of Studies. Don't be afraid to ask for help and remember that everyone was once in your shoes.

Get to know the school, spend some time looking at the teaching resources available. The schools' library of resource books can save you a lot of time planning classes. Above all, remember, as with any new situation, it gets easier very quickly. Most schools provide a program of induction training where you will meet the staff and have a tour of the school. You will also learn about the curriculum and types of courses you will be teaching, the course books used, administrative tasks, and methods of assessing students. There may also be some teaching workshops, particularly if the school follows its own methodology.

A teaching day is rarely 9am-5pm. Most business people and students can only study in the early morning, at lunch time, or after school or work. Consequently, teaching is often a split shift of a couple of classes in the morning, followed by a long break, and then a couple more classes in the evening. Most schools are also open on Saturdays. However, there may be days where you finish teaching by 11am. These types of hours can be difficult to get used to, but eventually you will fall into a rhythm and accept it as part of the job.

WILL I RECEIVE ANY FURTHER TRAINING?

Many schools, but not all, provide a program of ongoing training throughout your contract. This can include observations of your classes by the Director of Studies or a senior teacher, and seminars and workshops on teaching theory and practice.

WILL I SURVIVE FINANCIALLY?

TEFL salaries can vary greatly from country to country. In developing countries you can generally expect your salary to be high compared to the local average. This will give you enough to live very comfortably on, but not to save large amounts to take home with you. In developed countries, salaries are often similar, but of course with a much higher cost of living to deal with.

Many schools pay a monthly salary, usually based on an average number of teaching hours per week or per month, with extra for overtime. Others pay by the exact amount of hours you teach. The hourly rate can seem quite high, but remember that you are being paid for contact hours as well (usually 20 to 25 a week).

Country Guide

COUNTRY SPECIFIC INFORMATION
INTERNATIONAL SALARY SURVEY

Disclaimer

We have prepared this section of the guidebook to the best of our abilities. It is based on the body of information available to us from over 20 years of experience in this industry, online research, review of competitor literature, job boards, blogs, and actual contracts from our partner schools and recruiters. Please note that your actual salary, pay, or benefits may differ from the information presented but we believe that this information applies to the bulk of those going abroad. TEFL Institute does not employ any teachers abroad as such your final salary will be determined by your employer and not TEFL Institute.

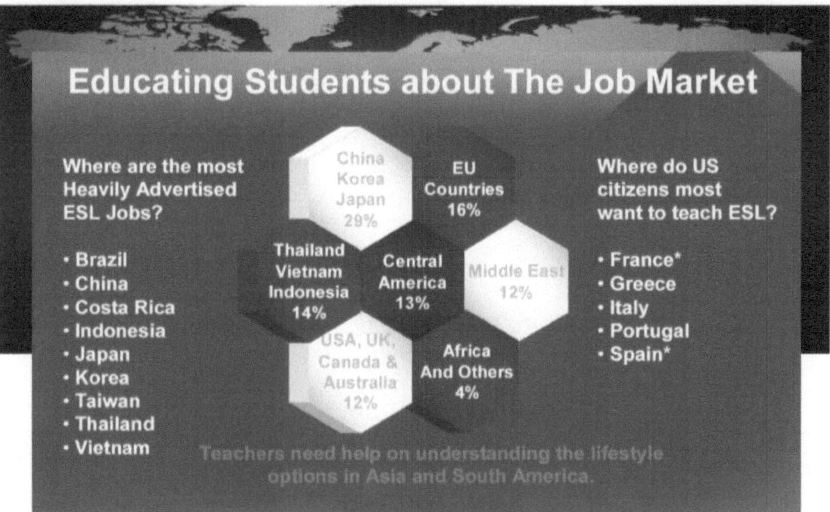

Country Guide

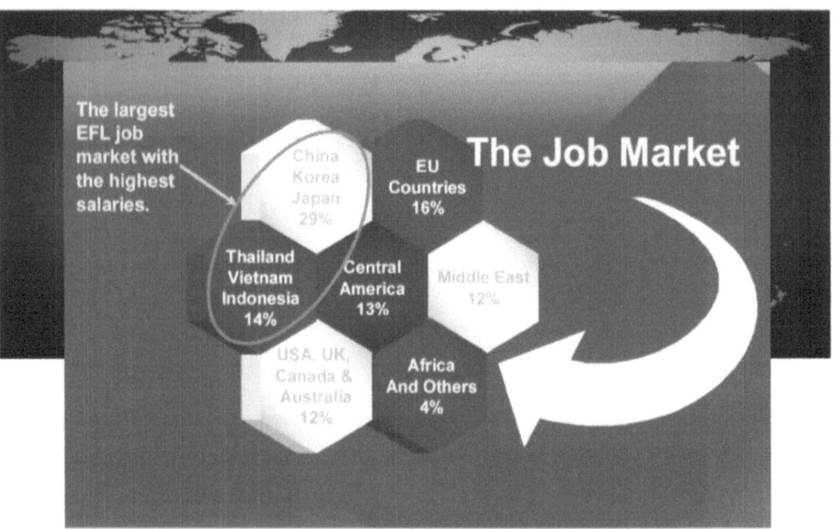

REGIONAL INFORMATION

Country Guide

JOBS IN ASIA: SOUTH KOREA, CHINA, TAIWAN, VIETNAM, JAPAN

Korea:

Age: 40 and under for private language institutes, 45 and under have opportunities in public schools with starting periods in March/April and August/September
Degree: 4 year degree needed
Citizenship: US, CA, NZ, UK, AU, SA
Hiring Period: Private language institutes year round, public schools March/April & August/ September

Recruiting agencies are used for job placement in Korea. There is no charge for their service.

TEFL Institute is the USA recruiting office for several Korean recruiting agencies. Our staff is well trained on hiring teachers for the Korean market. Our recruiters and staff can work with over 400 public and private schools throughout South Korea.

The recruiter emails job details to you, often sample contracts, job descriptions, hourly wages, vacation time, number of students, number of classes, and photos of the school.

You two will set up a time for a phone interview. They will want to hear your voice to determine if you are a native English speaker and will also ask you questions about when you want to go abroad. At this time, they will be able to answer your questions about contract details, housing, pay, logistics, etc.

If you want to accept the position then you will need to sign their contract and send hard copies of necessary documents to Korea via carrier (i.e., Federal Express). Typically both your official sealed transcript and your original university diploma (yes, the one in the frame). Please note the visa document requirements for Korea have become more specific in the last few years requiring notarizations and apostilles. Please check with TEFL Institute's Student Services Department and your schools in Korea for the most up to date requirements for the visa documents.

It will take at least 3 - 4 weeks for your documents to be approved by the Korean government after your school receives your package. In December of 2007 Korea established new visa requirements for the teaching visa. Candidates who are applying for a teaching visa must assemble the necessary documents including: transcripts, criminal background check and university diploma (original). You will be required to

notarize and apostille (internationally recognized notarization) some of these documents. Those who are applying for the teaching visa for Korea may also be required to complete an in-person interview at a Korean consulate in the US. Since visa requirements do change from time to time it is important to check with TEFL Institute's Student Services Department, the Korean consulate and your contracting school in Korea for the most up to date information.

Flights: You will arrange with your recruiter the date to fly into Korea. They should pick you up at the airport and take you to your apartment. After you settle in for a day or two, you will be taken to your school for orientation.

Flight reimbursement: Typically you will receive flight reimbursement within 2-3 weeks after starting your job. Please ask your school for specific details and refer to your contract as well.

Housing: Paid and typically furnished studios or single apartments are customary if you live alone. If you have a roommate you will each have your own bedroom. You should have this discussed and in writing prior to signing the contract. Typically an apartment comes with the basic necessities: bed, couch, chairs, tables, TV, utensils, and a western bathroom with a sit down toilet. The schools typically own the apartments and have them available for the new teachers. Most apartments are newer, usually less than 20 years old. Be sure to ask if utilities are included in the contract. Most apartments come with air conditioning but check since the summers can be very humid.

Bonus: Often jobs will present a 12 month completion bonus equal to one month's pay.

China:

Age: up to 60
Degree: 4 year degree needed for public schools and universities, 4 year degree needed for private language institutes in competitive areas like Shanghai and Beijing, no BA is available in some private language institutes outside of the larger cities
Citizenship: US, CA, NZ, UK, AU, SA
Hiring Period: All year except early February for 2 weeks during Chinese (Lunar) New Year, June and early July most schools are on vacation
Visa: If you have a BA, you will get a work visa ahead of time (time permitting)
Contract length: 6 or 12 months, summer language camps 1 – 2 months

The TEFL Institute can put you in touch directly with a school or recruiter in China.

Country Guide

Taiwan:

Age: 40 and under for private language institutes, 45 and under have opportunities in public schools with starting periods of March/April and August/September
Degree: 4 year degree needed
Citizenship: US, CA, NZ, UK, AU, SA
Contract length: 12 months
Hiring Period: All year

Taiwan is not recognized as a sovereign country. There is no Taiwan Embassy or consulate in the US, only representative offices. The school must send the documents to mainland Beijing, China for you to get a work visa. It is quite common for there to be a backlog of work permits. If you are leaving within a few months (especially if it is a September start), you will fly into Taiwan and work for 24 weeks on a tourist visa while the school is getting the paperwork back from China. Often jobs will present a 12 month completion bonus equal to one month's pay.

Vietnam:

Age: up to 40
Degree: 4 year degree
Citizenship: US, CA, NZ, UK, AU, SA
Hiring Period: All year except early February for 2 weeks during Chinese (Lunar) New Year
Contract length: 12 months

Many schools in Vietnam will only hire someone if they interview in person and on location. However, the schools we work with trust in our teacher's training and will interview over the phone and offer a contract. You may need to send a video tape of you teaching in advance along with your phone interview.

Housing is not provided but the school will assist in showing you where apartments are. Most jobs are in Ho Chi Minh City (Saigon) with some in Hanoi.

Most schools will provide you with work permit documentation to obtain your 12 month visa in advance.

Country Guide

Japan:

Age: up to 40
Degree: 4 year degree
Citizenship: US, CA, NZ, UK, AU, SA
*Citizens from other countries with documented 12 years of education in an English speaking school are also eligible for a work visa
Contract length: 12 months
Hiring Period: All year (Private language institutes year round, public schools March/April and August/September)

Most schools in Japan require an in person interview in the US. The TEFL Institute is an interviewer for many of the public schools in Japan. Start dates are March and September.

Most private language institutes interview throughout the year on location in the US. It is your responsibility to be professional, get yourself to an interview, and pass the screening. Job placement for Japan can be very competitive.

You are responsible for all fees associated with interviewing including travel to the interview site in the US. Major Japanese language schools have offices in Los Angeles, Chicago, New York, with occasional off site job hiring fairs throughout the country. Public school interviews are at various locations during the school year as well.

The job process typically involves the candidate to submit information directly through the school's corporate website, followed by a phone screening, in person interview and often video tape presentation of your teaching skills.

**Notes on year end bonuses for Asian countries: Make sure your contract is a 12 month contract, 365 days, not 11.5 months. Schools in Asia have been known to make your contract less than the 12 months in order to not pay the 12 month bonus.*

JOBS IN CENTRAL AND SOUTH AMERICA:

Latin America is known for a relaxed sense of style and business practices. Most countries will not offer work permits as it is costly in terms of money and time for the school. Most people will teach on a tourist permit and extend their stay by renewing their permit after 3 months or crossing the border for a few days and returning again under a new tourist visa. Each school has its own advice and customs on country policies. It is your responsibility to speak to the school about these details.

In Latin America people without a 4 year degree can find jobs in nearly every country. The TEFL Institute has direct contacts with many of the schools throughout the region. However, some of the country contacts will only take teachers with a 4 year degree. In Chile and Brazil our contacts will only take teachers with a 4 year degree but it has been known for people to get jobs in those countries without one. The TEFL Institute has contacts in Costa Rica, Argentina and Peru that will accept TEFL Institute graduates without this type of degree as well.

Most local schools will not hire teachers over 40 years old. However, American or British schools with franchises in Latin America are known to hire those older. The TEFL Institute can only offer placement to those 40 and under in most circumstances as this is dictated by our contacts.

Latin American schools are also open to hiring teachers from countries other than the United States, Canada, New Zealand, United Kingdom, Australia, and South Africa. A phone interview is always required for them to determine your verbal English skills. We can offer assistance with job contacts but ultimately they will determine if they will hire you based on your level of English fluency.

We can give advice for the major hiring seasons. There are always jobs available somewhere mid term but cannot be anticipated because of the contractual hiring cycles outlined below. Most schools in Latin America prefer to hire instructors in the country with an in-person interview. We advise you to contact schools in advance as well, but be prepared to apply in-person in the Latin American country of your choice. When applying in-person it is important to sync up with the peak hiring seasons which will vary by country. This period will have the most job openings. It is also important to coordinate your search in areas where there are many different language schools to choose from. Many instructors in Latin America will work at more than one school.

Almost all English students will be adults and many take language classes for their work advancement. If you wish to only work with children we can suggest the Ministry of Education program in Chile where you will be working in grade schools. This will be a rural assignment and will have a home stay.

Costa Rica:

Age: up to 40
Degree: BA preferred, no BA possible
Citizenship: United States, Canada, New Zealand, United Kingdom, Australia, South Africa preferred and other nationalities with English fluency accepted
Hiring Period: Best time of year – July & August, February & March
Contract length: 6 or 12 months

Location: San Jose has the majority of jobs. You may not get the full amount of hours during your first month to pay all your bills. The schools tend to test you out during this time to see how well you work with their clients.

Chile:

Age: up to 40
Degree: BA preferred, no BA possible
Citizenship: United States, Canada, New Zealand, United Kingdom, Australia, South Africa preferred and other nationalities with English fluency accepted
Hiring Period: Best time of year – July & August, February & March
Contract length: 6 or 12 months

Positions are available throughout Chile at both private language institutes and public schools. Some private language institutes will provide help securing a work visa. Public school positions are offered through the Ministry of Education in Chile. The Ministry offers contract positions of varying length including 8 weeks, 4 months, 6 months and 8 months. These contracts provide home stays, meals, visa help and a small stipend. See the Ministry of Education's website on page 93 for more information.

Country Guide

Peru:

Age: up to 40
Degree: No degree requirements
Citizenship: United States, Canada, New Zealand, United Kingdom, Australia, South Africa preferred and other nationalities with English fluency accepted
Hiring Period: Best time of year – July & August, February & March
Contract length: 6 or 12 months

If you take the Peru TEFL course you can start job placement immediately. Placement will be done with on location country interviews.

Argentina:

Age: up to 40
Degree: No degree requirements
Citizenship: United States, Canada, New Zealand, United Kingdom, Australia, South Africa preferred and other nationalities with English fluency accepted
Hiring Period: Best time of year – July & August, February & March
Contract length: 6 or 12 months

Most jobs are found in and around Buenos Aires. You will interview in person in Argentina. Most instructors work at more than one school to establish the necessary hours.

Brazil:

Age: up to 40
Degree: 4 year degree for TEFL Institute assistance
Citizenship: United States, Canada, New Zealand, United Kingdom, Australia, South Africa preferred and other nationalities with English fluency accepted
Contract length: 6 or 12 months
Hiring Period: Best time of year – July & August, late February & March

Jobs in the Sao Paulo and Belo Horizonte areas are available via TEFL Institute contacts. If you wish to explore other options we can refer you to a recruiting company that charges $250 and can arrange jobs in advance.

It is very common for people to teach on a tourist visa, about 98% of the teachers do so. The reason they do that is it is very expensive and time consuming for a school to

issue a work visa since teachers leave every 6 months or so. The work visa requirements have changed over the past year as well. This has made things very difficult for Americans to get a work permit as a result of the US demands on Brazilian nationals entering into the country.

JOBS IN EUROPE: WESTERN, CENTRAL EASTERN, EASTERN

Age: up to 55
Degree: 4 year degree for TEFL Institute assistance
Citizenship: Native English Speakers preferred
Contract length: 10-12 months
Hiring Period: September, January (Most schools have very few work hours available during July and August as most people are on vacation)

Western Europe (i.e. France, Spain, Italy, Germany, etc. in the EU):

Age: up to 55
Degree: 4 year degree for TEFL Institute assistance
Citizenship: Native English Speakers with EU citizenship preferred by employers for advance job offers and work legally
Contract length: 10 or 12 months
Hiring Period: September, January

Working for the Ministry of Education in France or Spain:

While the majority of instructors work at private language institutes, there are Ministry of Education programs available in both France and Spain. In France, the Teaching Assistant program accepts applications once a year for placement in public school positions throughout France. Experience with children, French language skills and prior teaching experience are a plus as the program is competitive. In Spain, the "Ambassadors" program accepts applications once a year for placement in public school positions throughout Spain. Experience with children, Spanish language skills and prior teaching experience are a plus as the program is competitive. Please note the Ministry of

Education Programs are able to offer visas and accept American applicants. This can be a great option for teaching in Europe.

European Union countries especially in the west (Spain, Italy, France, Germany, Greece) will prefer teachers to have EU citizenship as it is very difficult to obtain a work visa. If you have EU citizenship you can obtain a job in advance via a phone interview. Teachers who do not have EU citizenship (mostly Americans) will find many jobs available if they go to the country and interview in person and work for cash.

Spain:

Age: up to 55
Degree: 4 year degree for TEFL Institute assistance
Citizenship: Native English Speakers with EU citizenship preferred by employers for advance job offers
Contract length: 10 or 12 months
Hiring Period: September, January

The job market in Spain has many teachers therefore most teachers will work at several schools to make enough hours. Typically working 12-14 hours at two separate schools. Many Americans work in Spain but not legally.

Central and Eastern Europe:

Central and Eastern European countries, even in the EU, have a huge demand for English teachers (these countries previously spoke Russian as their second language). Work permits are easier to obtain when working with the schools. Non EU nationals can get work permits as well.

Czech Republic:

Age: up to 55 with some schools to 65
Degree: 4 year degree for TEFL Institute assistance
Citizenship: Native English Speakers with EU citizenship preferred by employers for advance job offers; US, CA, NZ, UK, AU, SA are able to get work permits
Contract length: 10 or 12 months
Hiring Period: September, January with some schools hiring all year
City: Prague

The school will help you transfer a tourist permit to a work permit while in the country within 90 days. Some schools may have housing arrangements, such as dorms or apartments for your initial stay. Some contracts provide housing, others do not.

Turkey:

Age: up to 55
Degree: 4 year degree for TEFL Institute assistance
Citizenship: US, CA, NZ, UK, AU, SA are able to get work permits
Contract length: 10 or 12 months
Hiring Period: September, January
Cities: Istanbul and Ankara have the highest demand

Schools can offer housing during your first few months. Visa procedures start in the US and finish in Turkey while you are there on a tourist visa.

FLIGHTS TO YOUR JOB WORLDWIDE:

You pay for your own flights to the country. China and South Korea typically will reimburse your flight.

HOUSING WORLDWIDE:

Often in a larger city, you will live in an apartment. You will be assisted to find an apartment by your school or you may share an apartment with another teacher. You pay for your own housing out of salary; the cost is up to you. Some schools may offer you a place to stay (apartment or dorm) for a few days to several months until you locate an apartment. You should be prepared to have money for a security deposit and first month's rent just as you would move in the US.

In a small city, the school will often arrange a home stay for you with a local family. You will have your own bedroom and share the home with a local family that is accustomed to foreign teachers. The housing cost will either be taken from your pay and forwarded to the family or you will pay the family directly.

Country Guide

WORK IN EUROPE
Teaching English Offers the Most Opportunities
By Susan Griffith

Whatever transatlantic trade agreements now exist or might exist in the future, one thing is sure: there will be no free exchange of labor between North America and Europe. As the ties between European nations strengthen, particularly among the members of the European Union, the employment opportunities for non-Europeans decline. Yet thousands of Americans live and work in Europe at this moment. Many of them have arrived in the past year and have found a niche, comfortable or otherwise.

The business of teaching English absorbs a considerable percentage of these temporary European residents. North Americans with a professional background in language teaching (e.g., a degree in applied linguistics and some relevant experience) might find an employer willing to sponsor them for a work visa. Even more desirable in many cases is a solid background in the business world. The majority of language teaching in Europe is to businessmen and women who want practical language tools for the workplace and prefer to be taught by someone with experience of this world than by a free-faced modern languages' graduate. Opportunities for non-Europeans are more plentiful in some countries than others—easier in Germany and Portugal than Italy and Spain, for example. The alternatives are to work for an employer who is not bothered about officialdom (this often implies a similarly casual approach to pay and working conditions) or to work on an informal or freelance basis. In European cities of any size the pool of native speaking teachers on the spot is so large that language school proprietors almost always have a choice of hopeful applicants to interview. In most cases a speculative application and resume sent from the U.S. will not meet with a favorable response.

Freelancing

The majority of North American language teachers and trainers in Europe work on a freelance basis. This can take the form of private tutoring whereby a native speaker goes it alone, finding private clients independently by advertising, etc. The more common way of freelancing, however, is to do it through an agency that provides language teaching, primarily to businesses. Freelancers work on short-term contracts or on an hourly basis. They are paid by the course or by the hour, but are not eligible for paid holidays or the other benefits of long-term employment. They must also worry about paying their own taxes plus they may have to pay compulsory contributions into a pension scheme (as in Germany) or to cover social security.

Country Guide

Independent freelance tutors will find it difficult to start teaching without contacts and a good working knowledge of the language. When they do get started, it may be difficult to earn a stable income because of the frequency with which pupils cancel. It is unrealistic for a newly arrived freelancer to expect to earn enough to live on in the first six months or so.

Getting clients for private lessons is a marketing exercise, and all the avenues that seem appropriate to your circumstances have to be explored. Here are some ways you can market yourself:

- Put a notice up in schools and universities, supermarkets or corner shops, and run an advertisement in the local paper if you have the use of a telephone.

- Send neat notices to local public schools, announcing your willingness to ensure the children's linguistic future.

- Compile a list of addresses of professionals (lawyers, architects, etc.) who may need English for their work and have the resources to pay for it. Then contact them.

- Call on export businesses, distribution companies, perhaps even travel agencies.

These methods should put you in touch with a few hopeful language learners. If you are good at what you do, word will spread and more paying pupils will come your way, though the process can be slow.

Working solo has disadvantages. Everyone, from lazy Greek teenagers to stressed Barcelona businessmen, cancels or postpones one-on-one lessons with irritating frequency. Since your clients are paying for your flexibility, you can't afford to take too tough a line. Unless your place is suitable for teaching, you will have to spend time traveling to your clients.

If you are more interested in integrating with the local culture than making money, exchanging conversation for board and lodging may be an appealing possibility. This can be arranged by answering (or placing) small ads in appropriate places. The American Church in Paris notice board is famous for this.

Language Schools

When you arrive in a likely place your initial steps might include some of the following: copy a list of schools from the yellow pages (many are now available online such as the Pages Jaunes in France or the Gelbe Seiten in Germany); read the classified columns of the local papers; check notice boards in locations such as universities, TEFL training centers, English language bookshops (where you should also notice which EFL materials are stocked), or places frequented by expatriate teachers.

After putting together a list of potential employers, get a detailed map and guide to the public transport network so you can locate the schools. Phone the schools and try to arrange a meeting with the director or academic director of studies. Even if an initial chat does not result in a job offer, you may learn something about the local TEFL scene that will help you at the next interview, especially if you ask lots of questions.

France: French Majors Encouraged to Apply

Advanced TEFL qualifications seem to be less in demand in France than business qualifications and experience or even just "commercial flair." Anyone who has a BA and is comfortable in a business setting has a chance of finding teaching work, particularly if they have a working knowledge of French.

The Cultural Service of the French Embassy – 4101 Reservoir Rd., NW, Washington, DC 20007, www.frenchculture.org runs an English Teaching Assistantship Program for US citizens. Postings last 69 months and are in primary or secondary schools or teacher training colleges. Assistants give conversation classes, provide classroom support and teach pupils about the U.S. A working knowledge of French is required so French majors are encouraged to apply. Assistants receive approximately 900 Euros gross per month.

Work permits must be obtained before leaving home, which is simply impracticable unless you have spent time in France and developed a working relationship with a cooperative employer. Note that the long-established Paris training organization, WICE, at 20 boulevard du Montparnasse www.wice-paris.org, can advise on how to get working papers, though it warns of the difficulties. Foreigners on a student visa are permitted to work 10-20 hours a week (after their initial year of study) or full-time in the vacations. At a more casual level, language exchanges for room and board are commonplace in Paris. These are usually arranged through advertisements or word of mouth. You can also offer English lessons privately in people's homes starting at 15-20 Euros a session.

Expatriate grapevines can be found all over Paris and are very helpful for finding teaching work and accommodations. The one in the foyer of the CIDJ at 101 Quai Branly (Métro Bir-Hakeim) is good for occasional student-type jobs, but sometimes there are ads for a soutien scolaire en Anglais (English tutor). It is worth arriving early to check for new notices (the hours are Monday-Friday 9:30 a.m. to 6 p.m. and Saturday mornings).

Other meccas for job-hunters include the American Church at 65 Quai d'Orsay and the American Cathedral in Paris at 23 av. George V. Both have notice boards crammed with employment opportunities, courses and housing listings. The Cathedral even offers career forums for job-seekers.

Highly qualified TEFL teachers from the U.S. might approach some of the important Paris companies such as Le Comptoir des Langues (63 Re la Boetie, 75008 Paris 01133145615356), and Executive Language Services (20 rue Sainte Croix de la Bretonnerie, 75004 Paris, 01133144 54 58 71 www.els-france.com), who between them employ over 100 teachers on a short or long-term basis.

Most expat meeting places in Paris distribute the free bilingual newsletter *France-USA Contacts* www.fusac.org that comes out every other Wednesday. Its classified ads are best followed up on the day the paper appears. It is also a good place to put your own "Work wanted" ad, which will cost $20 for 20 words. You can do this ahead of time by contacting FUSAC in the U.S. at P.O. Box 115, Coopers Station, New York, NY 10276 (212-777-5553, fax 212-777-5554).

An interesting development in the TEFL world is teaching by telephone, which is becoming more and more popular among language learners both for its convenience and for the anonymity. For many people, making mistakes over the phone is less embarrassing than face to face.

Apparently this method of teaching is great fun for teachers since the anonymity prompts people to spill out all their secrets. It is not necessary to be able to speak French, though you will need to have access to a computer and telephone. One company which specializes in this is Telab Cours de Langues par Telephone www.telab.com.

Country Guide

Germany: Business and IT Experience Can Help

Although Germany is a Eurocentric country, it is generally more tolerant of U.S. nationals working in certain sectors than its neighbors are, and that includes English teaching. People with a strong business or IT background and a knowledge of German might find their applications acceptable to the hundreds of language training companies in every German city, like Leipzig Language Service, Paul-List-Str. 8, 04103 Leipzig Tel./fax 0114934121112 82, artes@planet-interkom.de which employs a substantial number of native speakers. Both the Inlingua and Linguarama groups have an extensive network of schools and frequently post vacancies on their web sites www.inlingua.com and www.linguarama.com. For example, the Inlingua school in Munich employs about 30 native speakers for whom the minimum requirement is a university degree (Inlingua, Sendlinger-Tor-Platz 6, 80336 Munich; 011-49-89-231-15-30; muenchen@inlingua.de).

Speakers of American English will obviously have a better chance of finding teaching hours at an institute which caters to that market, like the German American Institute in Tubingen, Karlstrasse 3, 72072 Tubingen 011497071 795260 www.dai-tuebingen.de.

Adult education courses are offered throughout Germany at about 1,000 Volkhochschulen. English teachers must apply to the individual centers whose addresses are listed on the central web site www.vhs.de. Another major employer is Carl Duisberg Centren (Hansaring 49-51, 50670 Cologne 011492211626258 fki@cdc.de.) Students of German who would like to spend a year as an English language assistant in a German secondary school can contact the German organization that oversees the exchange, the Padagogischer Austauschdienst (Postfach 22 40, 53012 Bonn, 011 49 228 0228 501 0, www.kmk-pad.org). They distribute information on the teaching assistant program in Germany, which is also available through the Institute of International Education, 809 United Nations Plaza, New York, NY 10017-3580.

Greece: Permits Required, Difficult to Obtain

Fewer Americans teach in Greece because of visa difficulties. Non-European teachers need a teacher's license plus work and residence permits, and the Ministry of Education delays and often refuses to grant them. Americans of Greek extraction might consider claiming citizenship (while bearing in mind that this might make them liable to compulsory national service). A prospective teacher must obtain a letter of hire from the employer sent to an address outside Greece. The teacher then takes the letter to the

nearest Greek consulate and applies for a work permit, a procedure that takes at least two months. Detailed information about obtaining the correct documents are posted in the U.S. Embassy site www.usembassy.gov. Yet a number of schools, especially small ones in remote locations, may be prepared to tackle the bureaucratic procedures. Decisions are often based more on whether or not you hit it off with the interviewer than on your qualifications and experience, though a good university degree is essential.

The best times to look are early September, or possibly again at the beginning of January. Finding work in the summer in Athens is impossible.

It is normally necessary to knock on the doors of frontisteria, the private language crammers attended by the vast majority of secondary school students outside school hours. To find out about local frontisteria, contact the local branch of PALSO, the Pan-Hellenic Association of Language School Owners. By asking enough questions (try the local English language bookshop) you can find individual school addresses. The current monthly wage is the Euro equivalent of $650 gross. It should be possible to supplement wages with private tutoring at a rate of about $13-$15 an hour.

Spain: Market for English Teachers May Have Peaked
Recent years have seen unprecedented economic growth in Spain as business and industry forged ahead in the wake of European economic unification. Few job interviews would have omitted the question, "Can you speak English?" It seems now the market has peaked and the boom in English is over.

Work permit applications must be lodged in the applicant's country of residence and collected there as well, sometimes months later. Although teachers from outside the E.U. are occasionally hired on the spot by "store-front" schools and paid cash, the wage will normally be below the going rate. The area of the market that continues to grow is the teaching of children, starting with the pre-school age group. A knowledge of Spanish is virtually essential if you are going to teach young children (with whom the total immersion method is not really suitable).

The probable scenario for the new arrival is that he or she will elicit mild interest from one or two schools and will be told to contact the school again at the beginning of term when a few hours of teaching may be offered. Spanish students sign up for English classes during September and into early October; consequently, the academies do not know how many classes they will offer and how many teachers they will need until quite late. It can become a war of nerves – if you can afford to stay you have an increasingly good chance of becoming established.

Job-seekers in Madrid mainly rely on the Yellow Pages and the Madrid Blue Pages (a directory organized by street address). It is possible to pick out language schools in neglected neighborhoods this way, i.e., near where you are staying. It is also worth checking advertisements in the press, like La Vanguardia in Barcelona (especially the Sunday edition) and El Pais in Madrid. Alternatively, of course, you can simply wander the streets looking for schools. The density is so high that you are bound to come across them. Wherever you are looking for work, you can consult the Yellow Pages online at www.paginas-amarillas.es.

Several independent TEFL training organizations train large numbers of North Americans and acquiring an English language teaching certificate through one of these would be a good way of getting to know the local scene in Madrid or Barcelona (though the work permit problem persists). Investigate for example Via Lingua www.vialingua.org, who runs training courses in Madrid, Barcelona and Malaga, ITC English www.itc-training.com and Passport TEFL www.passportTEFL.com. Because schools run the whole gamut from prestigious to cowboy, every method of job-hunting works at some level. The big chains like Berlitz are probably a good bet for the novice teacher because of the stability of hours they can offer. Anyone hired by Berlitz receives a free week-long training course in the Berlitz Method. Similarly the Wall Street Institutes with scores of academies in Spain and a head office in Barcelona (Rambla de Catalunya 2-4, 2a Planta, 08007 Barcelona www.wallstreetinstitute.com) are always looking for teachers whom they train in their own method. One of the few organizations to favour U.S. nationals over Europeans is the IEN Institut Nord-america (Via Augusta 123, 08006 Barcelona www.ien.es) but to work for them you need at least two years of experience in teaching both adults and children and you must be prepared to wait 6-8 months for the work permit to be processed.

Many language schools and youth organizations run summer schools and camps for children and adolescents. For voluntary work as an English assistant at summer camps, try Relaciones Culturales, a youth exchange organization at Calle Ferraz 82, 28008 Madrid 01134915417103, fax 01134915591181, www.clubrci.es. They also place native speakers with Spanish families who want to practice English in exchange for providing room and board. Another agency involved in this sort of live-in placement is Castrum, Ctra. Ruedas 33, 47008 Valladolid 01134983222213 info@castrum.org, their placement fee is 160 Euros.

Portugal: Demand for Teachers Mostly in North

Unlike in Spain, some schools in Portugal claim to be willing to hire non-European nationals. According to official sources, once an American finds a teaching job in Portugal he or she can apply for the appropriate permits locally. After arrival, take the contract of employment to the local aliens office (Serviço de Estrangeiros e Fronteiras, www.sef.pt, —in Lisbon the SEF is at Avenida António Augusto Aguiar 20 011351213159681) or to the local police. The permit obtained here is sent off together with the contract of employment to the Ministry of Labor. The final stage is to take a letter of good conduct provided by the teacher's own embassy to the police for the work and resident permit.

Outside the cities, where there have traditionally been large expatriate communities, schools cannot depend on English speakers just showing up and so must recruit well in advance of the academic year. The demand for English teachers is mostly in the north. Apart from in the main cities of Lisbon and Oporto, jobs crop up in historic provincial centers such as Coimbra and Braga and in small seaside towns like Aveiro and Póvoa do Varzim. The small group Royal School of Languages (Av. Lourenco Peixinho 92-2°, Andar and Rua Jose Rabumba 2, 3800 Aveiro www.royalschooloflanguages.pt) employs about 30 teachers with TEFL certificates in their nine schools in small towns. These can be a welcome destination for teachers burned out from teaching in big cities or first-time teachers who want to avoid the rat race. Both the main cities of Lisbon and Oporto have American Language Institutes which prefer to employ teachers from the U.S. The ALI in Lisbon can be contacted at ali@mail.telepac.pt.

Italy: Work Permits Difficult to Obtain

Red tape is most daunting in Italy, and work permits are virtually impossible for non-E.U. citizens to obtain. There is a pronounced bias towards hiring Britons as indicated by the names of the main language school chains, the British Schools Group, British Colleges, British Institutes, Oxford Schools. Yet there are also those willing to hire qualified Americans, such as the Interlingue School of Languages in Rome (www.interlingue-it.com, Via E. Q. Visconti 20, 00193 Rome 0113906321 5740).

Yet enrollment in English language schools continues to increase at a dramatic rate among ordinary Italians, and there will always be schools that choose not to comply with the very strict labor regulations. Milan is considered a promising destination, even for unqualified non-Europeans. Yet it is not just the sophisticated urbanites of Rome, Florence, and Milan who long to learn English. Small towns in Sicily and Sardinia, in the Dolomites, and along the Adriatic all have more than their fair share of private language schools and institutes. As in Spain, a number of organizations run language summer

camps, among them ACLE Summer & City Camps, Via Roma 54, 18038 San Remo tel./fax 011390184 506070 www.acle.org. Summer counsellors must enroll in a short training course for 150 Euros and are paid 170-190 Euros per week plus board and accommodation. Summer counsellors and language tutors aged 19-28
are recruited for Italian camps by the Canadian company Scotia Personnel Ltd., www.scotia-personnel-ltd.com.

Italy has a complete range of language schools, as the heading Scuole di Lingue in any Yellow Pages will confirm. The Pagine Gialle can be consulted on www.paginegialle.it. At the elite end of the market, there is a handful of schools (35 at present) which belong to AISLI, the Associazione Italiana Scuole di Lingua Inglese, administered from Via Campanella 16, 41100 Modena, www.eaquals.org. Strict regulations exclude all but ultra-respectable schools.

Another possibility is to set up as a freelance tutor, though a knowledge of Italian is even more an asset here than is knowing the local language elsewhere in Europe. You can post notices in supermarkets, tobacconists, and primary and secondary schools. It may be worth advertising in a local paper.

TEACHING ENGLISH IN PORTUGAL
The Easiest Western European Country in Which to Find Work
By Risa Barkan

Americans with TEFL certification find Portugal to be the easiest Western European country in which to find work as an English teacher. However, most schools won't hire teachers without a certificate unless they have considerable previous teaching experience.

You can also find private students by putting signs up in the embassies. Many expatriates living in Lisbon would like to improve their English.

Although tourist visas expire after 60 days, my school gave me a letter to take to the Misterio de Finances to extend my stay for the duration of my nine-month contract. (It takes about a year to be approved for a work permit. I would suggest going through the process only if you plan to stay longer than one year.)

Schools

- Centro de Linguas, www.cial.pt, Av. República, 41 - 2º, 1000, Lisbon, Ph: 011351213533733, Fax: 011351213523096, cialis@mail.telepac.pt. Specializes in teaching business English in companies. Pays for transportation and free Portuguese lessons for all levels. Pays about $800 per month on contract for first-year teachers (part-time work is also possible). The pay is enough to live on however, for extras, bring savings from home.

- American Language Institute, Av. Duque de Loule, 22-1, 1050, Lisbon, Ph: 01135113146107, Fax: 01135113524848. Pays approximately $20 per hour for teaching general English to all levels.

- International House, www.ihlisbon.com, Rua Marquês Sá da Bandeira, 16, 1050, Lisbon, Ph: 00351213151493, Fax: 00351213530081, info@ihlisbon.com.

Some other places to contact are the British Council, Cambridge Schools, and Oxford Schools, all of whom have branches throughout the country.

List of Job Boards and Websites

JOB BOARDS AND RESOURCES FOR TEACHING ESL OVERSEAS

- Transitions Abroad: http://www.transitionsabroad.com
- AAC's ESL Job Circle: http://www.aacircle.com.au/esljobcircle.htm
- ESL Cafe's International Job Board: www.eslcafe.com/joblist
- ESL Job Feed: www.esljobfeed.com
- ESL Job Find: www.esljobfind.com
- ESL Teachers Board: www.eslteachersboard.com
- Linguistic Funland: www.tesol.net/jobs
- Mark's ESL World: www.marksesl.com
- TeachOverseas.ca: www.teachoverseas.ca
- TESall.com: http://www.tesall.com/esl-tesol-jobs/
- TEFL.com: www.tefl.com
- TEFL.net's ESL Job Offers: www.tefl.net/jobs/jobs.pl

MINISTRY OF EDUCATION PROGRAMS AROUND THE WORLD

Ministry of Education Programs are offered in a variety of countries around the world. Please the visit the program websites for specific details. These programs accept applications and interview on set schedules each year. If you are interested in one of the Ministry of Education Programs listed below be sure to research and plan in advance.

- JET - Japan Exchange Teaching Program: http://www.jetprogramme.org/
- EPIK – English Program In Korea: http://www.epik.go.kr/
- Chilean English Opens Doors Program:
http://www.puntonorte.cl/voluntarios/programs/full-time/
- France Teaching Assistant Program:
http://www.frenchculture.org/assistantshipprogram
- Spain Ambassador's Program:
http://www.mec.es/sgci/usa/en/programs/us_assistants/default.shtml

List of Job Boards and Websites

ESL TEACHING NEWS AND COMMENTARY

- The TESall Ticker: http://www.tesall.com/tesl-tefl-tesol-courses/
- ELT News: www.eltnews.com
- EL Gazette: www.elgazette.com
- ET Professional: www.etprofessional.com
- Guardian TEFL: www.guardian.co.uk/education/tefl

ESL TEACHER TRAINING INFORMATION AND ORIENTATION

- Transitions Abroad: http://www.transitionsabroad.com
- ESL Cafe Teacher Training Forum: www.eslcafe.com/discussion/dz1/
- Go Teach TESOL Primer: www.goteach.ca/tesol.html
- TESall.com's Course Catalog: http://www.tesall.com/tesl-tefl-tesol-courses/
- Cactus TEFL: www.cactustefl.com
- EI's Your TEFL Training Options: www.english-international.com/training.html
- Linguistic Funland: www.tesol.net/teslprog.teach.html
- TEFL.com's Which Course?: www.whichcourse.com
- Free Graduate TESOL Guide: www.matesol.info

ESL DISCUSSION FORUMS

- ESL Café Job Discussion Forum: www.eslcafe.com/forums/job/index.php
- EnglishForums.com: www.englishforums.com
- TEFL.net: www.tefl.net/forums/index.php
- EFL-Law: www.efl-law.com
- TESall.com's Job Discussion Forum: http://tesall.com/esl-tesol-teachers/

ESL LESSON PLANS AND CLASSROOM RESOURCES

- English Raven: www.englishraven.com/Main.html
- MES English.com: www.mesenglish.com
- ESL Lounge.com: www.esllounge.com
- English4u.com: www.english4u.com

List of Job Boards and Websites

- Breaking News English Daily: www.breakingnewsenglish.com
- Speak Read Write: www.speak-read-write.com
- Boggle's World: www.bogglesworldesl.com
- Developing Teachers.com: www.developingteachers.com
- ESLgo.com: www.eslgo.com
- TESall.com: www.tesall.com/esl-tesol-lessons

WORLDWIDE PORTALS, WEBSITES, AND RESOURCES FOR TEACHING ENGLISH ABROAD

- English Job Maze, www.englishjobmaze.com, lists ESL/EFL jobs and provides resources on how to become a teacher. See their excellent country-by-country breakdown of ESL trends.

- EnglishClub.com, www.englishclub.com, provides an excellent ESL/EFL links directory, which contains extensive collections of resources for both teachers and students alike.

- eslbase.com, www.eslbase.com, has new job opportunities daily, as well as a worldwide directory of TEFL courses, downloadable resources for teachers, and a "Find an old TEFL friend" service.

- Dave's ESL Cafe, www.eslcafe.com, ESL Cafe's Web Guide: Jobs, www.eslcafe.com/search/Jobs by Dave Sperling. This site has a staggering amount of well-organized information about teaching English as a second language, either abroad or in the U.S., as well as job databases. Useful for those with and without TESL credentials. A highly recommended resource for anyone interested in working abroad.

- ESL Job Find, www.esljobfind.com. ESL Job Find connects Employers and Job Seekers worldwide. They have ESL job listings for Korea, Japan, China and Taiwan in Asia, and other locations such as Europe and South America.

- Fulbright English Teaching Assistantships, www.us.fulbrightonline.org/thinking_teaching.html. Program for recent university graduates to serve as English Teaching Assistants in various locations around the world including Belgium/Luxembourg, France, Germany, Hungary, Korea,Taiwan and Turkey.

List of Job Boards and Websites

▶ GlobalStudy, www.globalstudy.com. Guide to international education, including message boards and a directory of English language school websites in the United States, Canada, Great Britain, Ireland, Australia and New Zealand.

▶ Peace Corps, www.peacecorps.gov. Sometimes overlooked because of its designation as a volunteer program. Peace Corps is one of the largest work abroad programs for U.S. citizens. It provides some of the best paid teaching opportunities in less wealthy regions in Africa, Latin America, Asia, and Europe.

▶ Randall's ESL Cyber Listening Lab, www.esl-lab.com. This free multimedia site is designed to help English learners improve their listening comprehension through a variety of audio and video conversations, interviews, and news reports. Randall Davis is the developer of this site, and he has written, recorded, and edited the materials as an independent project at his home in the USA.

▶ Teachers of English to Speakers of Other Languages (TESOL), www.tesol.org. Web site of the largest U.S. professional association for ESL teachers. An essential resource for qualified professionals, though less useful for students.

▶ T.E.F.L. Board, www.teflboard.org, a site dedicated solely to the presentation of curriculum and program details on E.S.L. teacher training certificate courses and diploma programs all over the world.

▶ TEFL.NET, www.tefl.net, offers a TEFL Course Database, TEFL Jobs Center, TEFL Help Desk, ESL lesson plans and other teaching resources to teach English as a foreign or second language.

▶ TEFL Professional Network, www.tefl.com, has a huge online database of ESL jobs.

▶ TESL/TEFL/TESOL/ESL/EFL/ESOL Links, iteslj.org/links, is a no-nonsense compilation of links for students and teachers.

▶ TESall.com, www.tesall.com, is the first vertical search portal for ESL/TEFL jobs and TransitionsAbroad.com's favorite job search site.

▶ Univ. of Michigan, International Center's Overseas Opportunities Office, www.umich.edu/~icenter/swt/work/options/index.html. See article on "Teaching Abroad Without Certification" which lists U.S. based programs for teaching abroad

List of Job Boards and Websites

PORTALS AND WEBSITES BY REGION/COUNTRY FOR TEACHING ENGLISH ABROAD

▶ Australia Academic Circle (AAC), www.aacircle.com.au , is a portal for teaching English in Taiwan, Korea, Japan or China as well as Europe. The site provides ESL job boards and country profiles which discuss visa info, accommodations, taxes and TESL / TEFL courses.

▶ Ajarn.com, www.ajarn.com. Job postings, resources and a discussion forum on teaching English in Thailand and issues surrounding.

▶ Asiapond.com, www.asiapond.com, is a simple online jobs pool for teaching in Asia.

▶ BENZHI, www.benzhi.com. Asian EFL job community.

▶ BigDaikon, www.bigdaikon.com. Focuses mainly on JET Ministry of Education positions but includes useful information for living and working as an English teacher in Japan.

▶ Bogglesworldesl.com, bogglesworldesl.com/esl_jobs.htm. Job listings for China, Korea, and Japan.

▶ China TEFL Network, www.chinatefl.com/indexe.asp, is a portal for jobs teaching English in China.

▶ Expatriate Café, www.expatriatecafe.com, has morphed from its focus on the ESL community in Spain towards being an excellent general expatriate community site for Spain.

▶ GaijinPot, www.gaijinpot.com. Focuses on all things Japan including jobs, discussion forums, housing, living and points of interest. It is a fantastic site for research on teaching English in Japan.

▶ Inglesnet.com. The most complete guide for EFL learners in Argentina and Latin America. It provides very useful information, interesting links, complete directories of national and international English teaching institutions and a lot more.

List of Job Boards and Websites

- Internet Works: Teach English in Mexico, www.teach-english-mexico.com, provides a one-stop-shop for information and resources on teaching English in Mexico.

- Jobs in Japan, www.jobsinjapan.com, has loads of ESL job postings.

- MadridTeacher.com, www.madridteacher.com. A site for teachers in Madrid, Spain, to advertise their services and to exchange information about the local teaching market on the Forum.

- Mekong ESL, www.mekongesl.com, has ESL opportunities in Cambodia, Laos and Vietnam.

- OHayo Sensei, www.ohayosensei.com. Listings of ESL and other types of teaching positions in Japan.

- Teach English in Poland, www.teachpoland.com. Job boards listing English language teaching jobs in Poland.

- TEFL ASIA, www.teflasia.com, is an excellent portal for Asian ESL jobs, articles and resources.

- TESOL FRANCE, www.tesolfrance.org, represents the interests of professionals in EFL (English as a Foreign Language) in France.

www.ingramcontent.com/pod-product-compliance
Ingram Content Group UK Ltd.
Pitfield, Milton Keynes, MK11 3LW, UK
UKHW041929190726
13854UKWH00004B/1531

9 780557 665587